Historical Thinking Skills Workbook

John P. Irish

Carroll Senior High School, Southlake, Texas

W. W. Norton & Company has been independent since its founding in 1923, when William Warder Norton and Mary D. Herter Norton first published lectures delivered at the People's Institute, the adult education division of New York City's Cooper Union. The firm soon expanded their program beyond the Institute, publishing books by celebrated academics from America and abroad. By midcentury, the two major pillars of Norton's publishing program— trade books and college texts— were firmly established. In the 1950s, the Norton family transferred control of the company to its employees, and today—with a staff of four hundred and a comparable number of trade, college, and professional titles published each year—W. W. Norton & Company stands as the largest and oldest publishing house owned wholly by its employees.

Director of High School Publishing: Jenna Bookin Barry
Project Editor: Melissa Atkin
Editorial Assistant: Aimee Lam
Managing Editor, College: Marian Johnson
Managing Editor, College Digital Media: Kim Yi
Production Manager: Sean Mintus
Composition: Westchester
Manufactured in the United States by RR Donnelley

ISBN 978-0-393-26495-1 (pbk.)

W. W. Norton & Company, Inc., 500 Fifth Avenue, New York, NY 10110-0017

wwnorton.com

W. W. Norton & Company Ltd., Castle House, 75/76 Wells Street, London W1T 3QT

2   3   4   5   6   7   8   9   0

*AP and Advanced Placement program are registered trademarks of the College Board, which was not involved in the production of, and does not endorse, this product. Reprinted by permission of the College Board.

John P. Irish received his B.A. in philosophy and political science from Southern Methodist University, his M.A. in philosophy from the University of Arkansas, and a M.L.S. in American Studies from Southern Methodist University. He is currently working on his Doctorate in Humanities from SMU. He has been teaching U.S. History for over 15 years. He currently teaches AP U.S. History at Carroll Senior High School, in Southlake, Texas, where he coaches the UIL Social Studies team and is the UIL Academic Coordinator.

Contents

Contextualization and Synthesis

Turning Points

Continuity and Change over Time

Argumentation

Chronological Reasoning

Preface

The idea for this workbook was born on Wednesday, May 14, 2014. As I sat in an empty classroom while my students were busily taking the AP* U.S. History exam, I thought about how my classroom would function differently under the redesigned course in the coming years. I would still be teaching American history, so there would be few content changes. The students would still be required to write Document Based Questions (DBQs) and Free Response Questions (FRQs), which are now called Long Essays (LEs), and they would still have those pesky things known as Short Answer Questions (SAQs). There would be themes, but we have always had themes in the AP U.S. History course. Then it hit me: The historical thinking skills are the new component of the exam. While we have always been responsible for addressing historical skills, they would now be an explicit, essential component of both the assessment and pedagogy going forward under the redesign.

Teachers can use these graphic organizers in a number of different ways. But if you simply hand them out to your students, sit at your desk, and collect them at the end of the period, then you are not utilizing them in the best possible way. These graphic organizers should be used to help students conceptualize the specific historical content under investigation. First, allow students time to digest the content independently, then as a class, ask students to share their thoughts or conclusions. Collaborate as a class to complete the worksheets, not always but often allowing students to interact with their peers while they discuss the topics with each other. Challenge the class by using Socratic questioning to make students think and rethink their positions. Have students challenge each other to incite debates.

These graphic organizers have helped tremendously to make my classroom more student-centered. I was never much of a lecturer, but now I am truly becoming a facilitator of learning. At the same time, I am helping my students prepare and succeed on the AP U.S. History exam. I use these graphic organizers as a way to get students writing, which is a critical skill for students to be successful on the exam—as well as in college and life. I use these worksheets to assign follow-up or remediation activities for individual students. I ask students to develop their own thesis statements based on their conclusions for the worksheets' activities, especially since most of these activities resemble essay prompts from the AP U.S. History exam. Thus, you can use this resource to touch on all three elements of the redesigned course: content, skills, and writing. None of these things exist inside a vacuum, and none are mutually exclusive. In fact, how would someone teach these historical thinking skills without reinforcing the content? How would someone teach writing without reinforcing the content and the relevant skills?

There are a number of folks I would like to thank for all their help and encouragement with this workbook.

Jenna Bookin Barry and Melissa Atkin at W. W. Norton & Company. Jenna showed confidence in me when I approached her with this idea, and Melissa has been an outstanding editor. This workbook would not be here if not for them. They have been great to work with and confirmed my decision to go with Norton for publication of this workbook.

All my former, present, and future students (both in my AP U.S. History classes as well as all my teacher trainings). They have been the source of motivation and ideas for this workbook. They also served, in many instances, as the first test cases for most of these activities. They helped actualize these lessons.

My parents, Johnny and Sandra Irish. They encouraged me to go into education; and if not for them, I would not be the person I am today. They taught me to love working with students, and that has resulted in my current career choice. I have the best job in the world and for that I am eternally thankful to them. Dad has been a rock of support over this entire process, and I appreciate him more than words can describe.

My wife, Elizabeth Irish. She encouraged me from the start with this idea, supported me when things seemed down, tested most of these activities in her own classroom, and offered valuable feedback and suggestions when the activities needed improvements. I also am appreciative of her understanding when I was pounding away on the computer working on this book when I could have, and probably should have been, doing other things with her and the pets.

To all of these folks I say, thank you!

Student Instructions: Causation

When we are asked to identify the historical causation of an event, we are, essentially, being asked to identify the events that led up to the historical event under investigation as well as the results of the historical event under investigation. There can be both long-term and short-term causes and effects. Long-term events are those events that are further away from the historical event under investigation, and short-term events are those events that are more immediate to the historical event under investigation.

The purpose of these Causation graphic organizers is to investigate the causes and effects of different events in American history. On the surface it may appear easy to identify different causes and effects, however, upon closer examination, it might be surprising to see certain events having stronger causal connections than others. It is also important to practice identifying long-term versus short-term causes and effects and evaluating the most and least important causes and effects of historical events.

The first graphic organizer in this category has been completed in order to serve as a model. Notice that there is a variety of ways in which the causes and effects can be investigated. For instance, in this sample worksheet, the student chose Ideology, Politics, and Economics as the three categories of investigation, but there could have been an infinite number of categories chosen. There is no right or wrong answer here, but there are some answers that might be easier to work with than others.

Causation: War of 1812

CAUSE	EFFECT

Ideology

- War Hawks
- Continued belief that the U.S. was not independent from England

→

Ideology

- Defeated the British a second time
- Strong sense of nationalism

Politics

- American Indian presence on the western front

→

Politics

- Death of the Federalists
- Removal of British presence in North America
- Rise of Andrew Jackson

Economics

- Impressment of American sailors
- Embargo Act
- Discruption of trade/commerce

→

Economics

- Rise of the Market Revolution
- Increase of American industry and commerce
- Economic independence

Most Important and Why?

Cause: Economics—lack of trade prohibited the country from growing like it needed to

Effect: Ideology—growth of nationalism led to many other developments and led to the Era of Good Feelings

Least Important and Why?

Cause: Politics—American Indians were not a real threat

Effect: Politics—Federalists were strong, but other opposition parties took their place

Causation: European Exploration

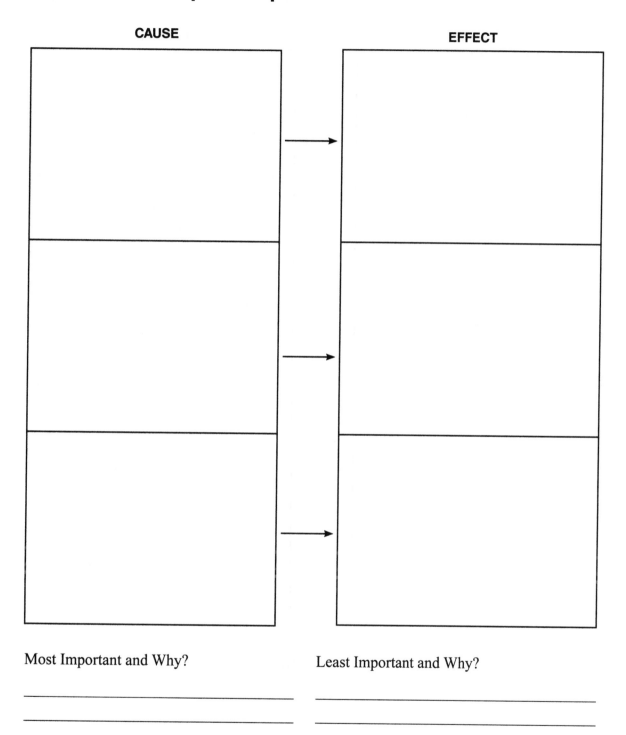

CAUSE

EFFECT

Most Important and Why?

Least Important and Why?

_____   _____
_____   _____
_____   _____
_____   _____
_____   _____

Causation: English Colonization

CAUSE	EFFECT

Most Important and Why?

Least Important and Why?

_____

_____

_____

_____

Causation: American Slavery

CAUSE	EFFECT

Most Important and Why?

Least Important and Why?

_____

_____

_____

_____

_____

Causation: Growth of Colonial America

CAUSE	EFFECT

Most Important and Why?

_____
_____
_____
_____

Least Important and Why?

_____
_____
_____
_____

Causation: First Great Awakening

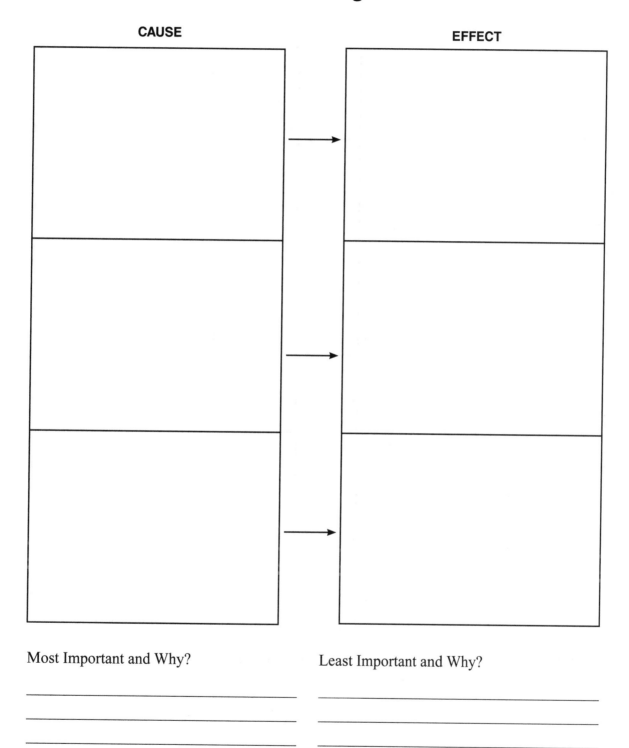

CAUSE

EFFECT

Most Important and Why?

Least Important and Why?

_____   _____

_____   _____

_____   _____

_____   _____

Causation: French and Indian War

CAUSE	EFFECT

Most Important and Why?

_____

_____

_____

_____

Least Important and Why?

_____

_____

_____

_____

Causation: American Revolution

CAUSE	EFFECT

Most Important and Why?

_____

_____

_____

_____

_____

Least Important and Why?

_____

_____

_____

_____

_____

Causation: Ratification of the U.S. Constitution

CAUSE	EFFECT

Most Important and Why?

_____

_____

_____

_____

Least Important and Why?

_____

_____

_____

_____

Causation: Election of 1800

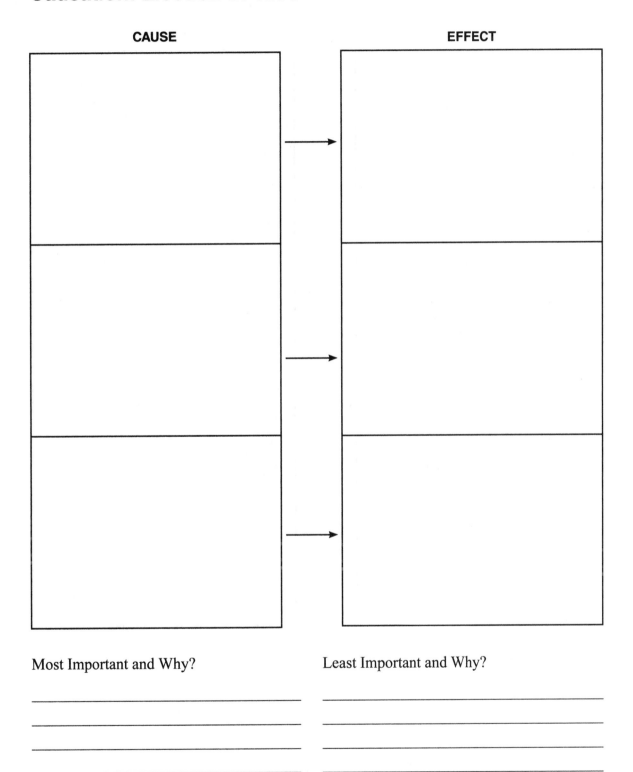

CAUSE

EFFECT

Most Important and Why?

_____
_____
_____
_____
_____

Least Important and Why?

_____
_____
_____
_____
_____

Causation: Market Revolution

CAUSE		EFFECT
	→	
	→	
	→	

Most Important and Why?

_____
_____
_____
_____
_____

Least Important and Why?

_____
_____
_____
_____
_____

Causation: American Slave Culture

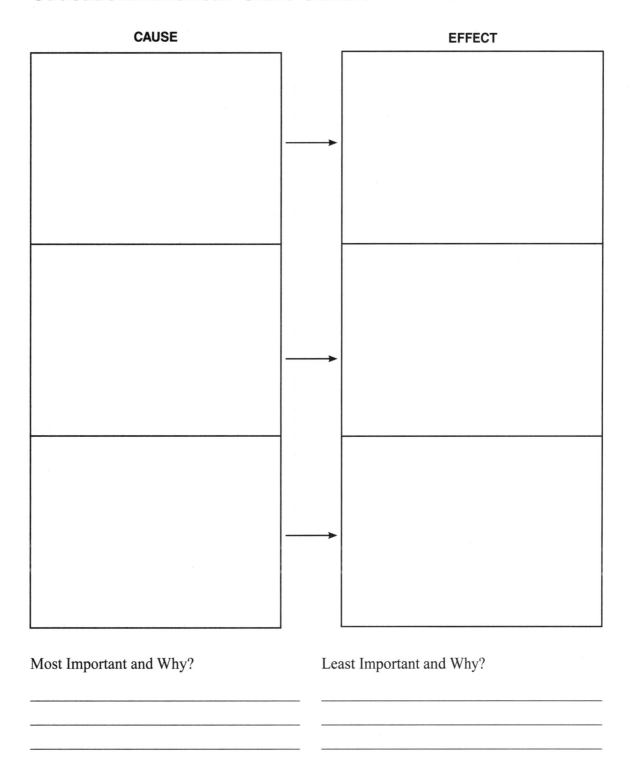

CAUSE

EFFECT

Most Important and Why?

_____
_____
_____
_____
_____

Least Important and Why?

_____
_____
_____
_____
_____

Causation: Religious Reformers

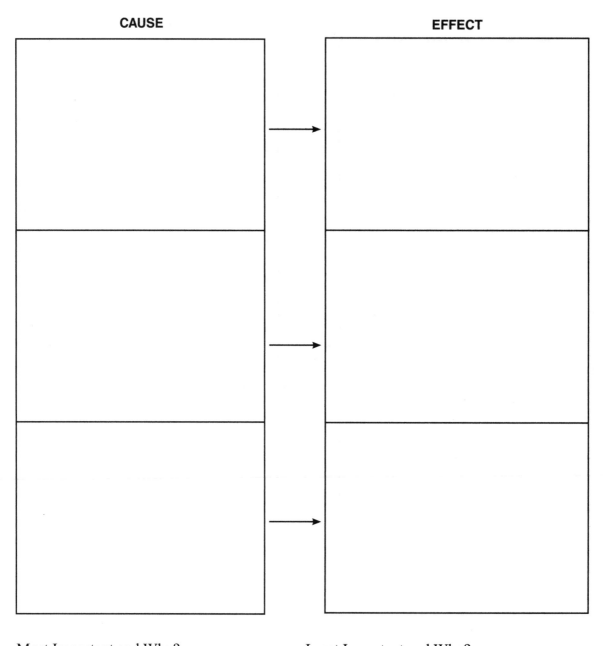

CAUSE

EFFECT

Most Important and Why?

_____
_____
_____
_____
_____

Least Important and Why?

_____
_____
_____
_____
_____

Causation: Manifest Destiny

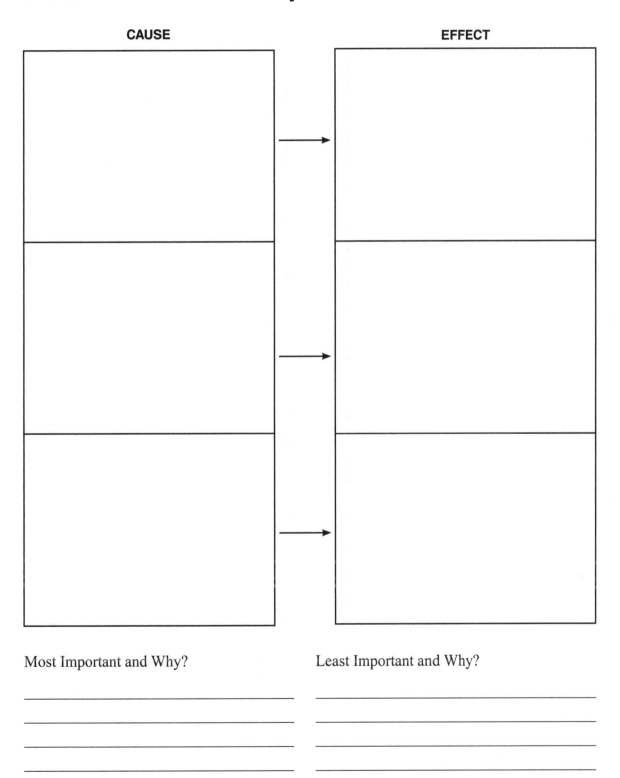

CAUSE

EFFECT

Most Important and Why?

_____
_____
_____
_____

Least Important and Why?

_____
_____
_____
_____

Causation: American Civil War

CAUSE	EFFECT

Most Important and Why?

_____
_____
_____
_____
_____

Least Important and Why?

_____
_____
_____
_____
_____

Causation: Radical Reconstruction

CAUSE	EFFECT

Most Important and Why?

_____

_____

_____

_____

Least Important and Why?

_____

_____

_____

_____

Causation: Second Industrial Revolution

CAUSE		EFFECT
	→	
	→	
	→	

Most Important and Why?

Least Important and Why?

_____ _____

_____ _____

_____ _____

_____ _____

_____ _____

Causation: Populism

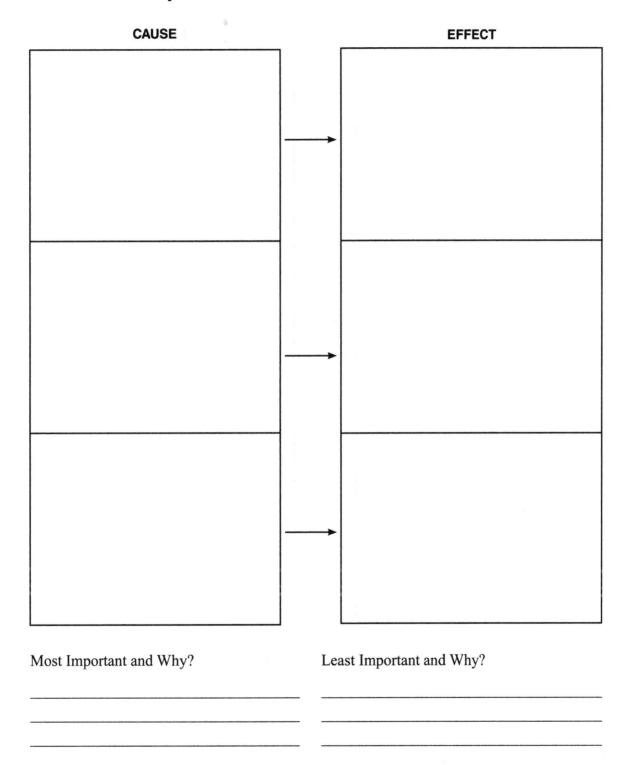

CAUSE

EFFECT

Most Important and Why?

_____
_____
_____
_____
_____

Least Important and Why?

_____
_____
_____
_____
_____

Causation: New Imperialism

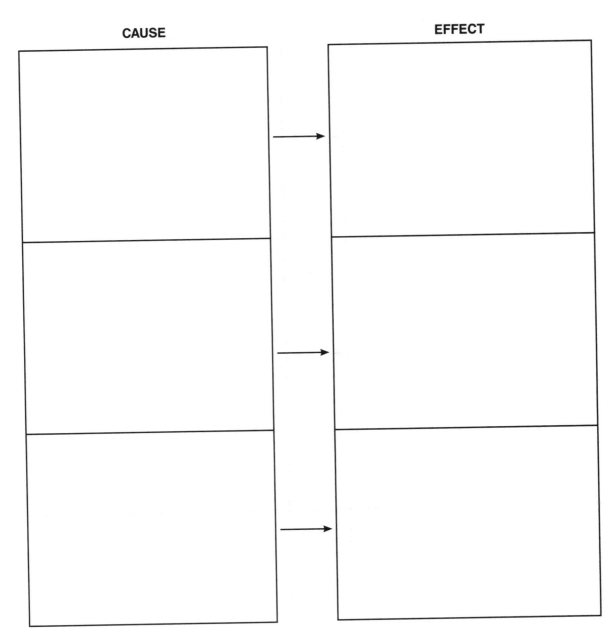

CAUSE

EFFECT

Most Important and Why?

Least Important and Why?

_____
_____
_____
_____
_____

_____
_____
_____
_____
_____

Causation: Progressivism

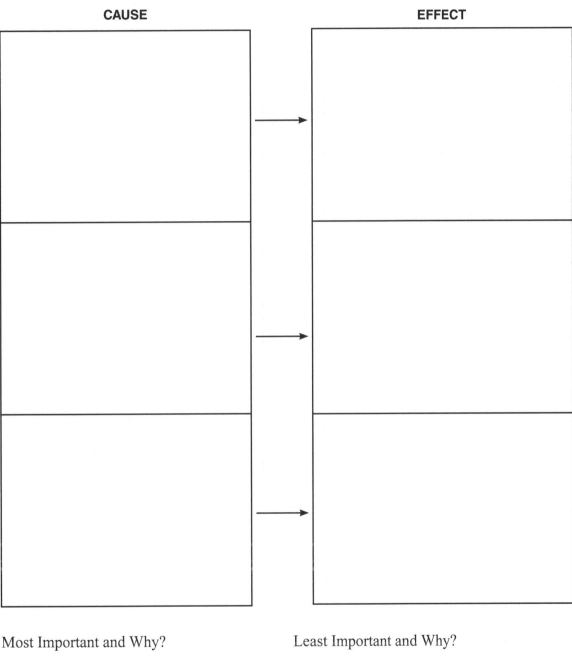

CAUSE

EFFECT

Most Important and Why?

Least Important and Why?

_____   _____
_____   _____
_____   _____
_____   _____
_____   _____

Causation: American Involvement in WWI

CAUSE	EFFECT

Most Important and Why?

_____
_____
_____
_____
_____

Least Important and Why?

_____
_____
_____
_____
_____

Causation: 1920s Consumerism

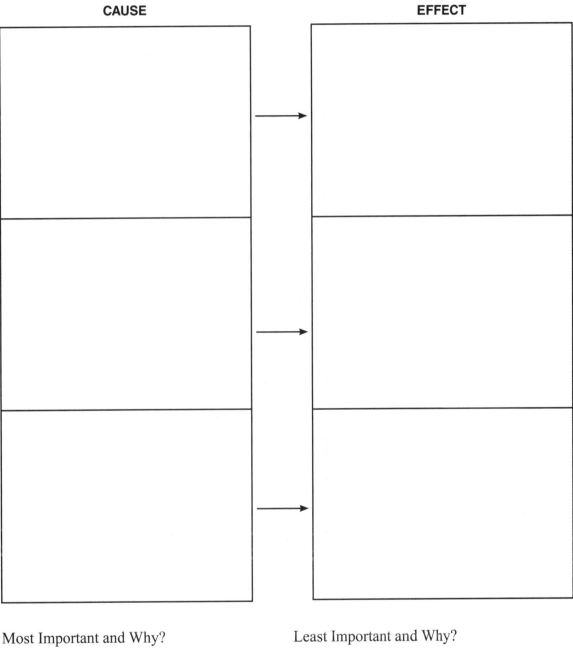

CAUSE

EFFECT

Most Important and Why?

_____
_____
_____
_____
_____

Least Important and Why?

_____
_____
_____
_____
_____

CA22

Causation: 1920s Culture Wars

CAUSE	EFFECT

Most Important and Why?

_____
_____
_____
_____
_____

Least Important and Why?

_____
_____
_____
_____
_____

Causation: New Deal

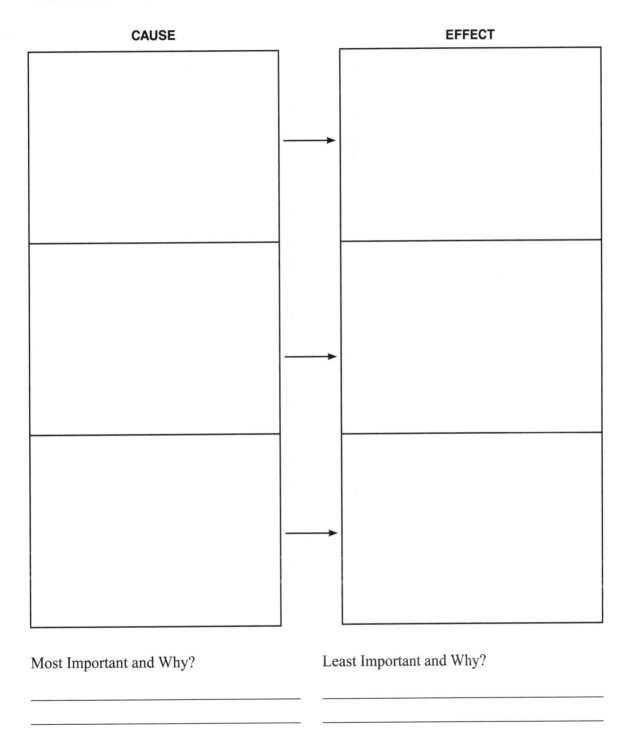

CAUSE

EFFECT

Most Important and Why?

Least Important and Why?

Causation: American Involvement in WWII

CAUSE   **EFFECT**

Most Important and Why?

Least Important and Why?

_____   _____
_____   _____
_____   _____
_____   _____
_____   _____

Causation: Cold War

CAUSE   **EFFECT**

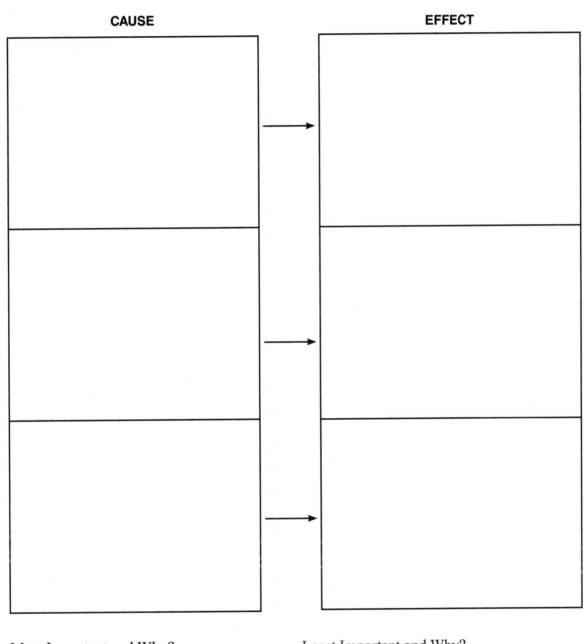

Most Important and Why?

_____

_____

_____

_____

_____

Least Important and Why?

_____

_____

_____

_____

_____

CA26

Causation: 1950s Consumerism

CAUSE	EFFECT

Most Important and Why?

_____
_____
_____
_____
_____

Least Important and Why?

_____
_____
_____
_____
_____

Causation: Counter Culture

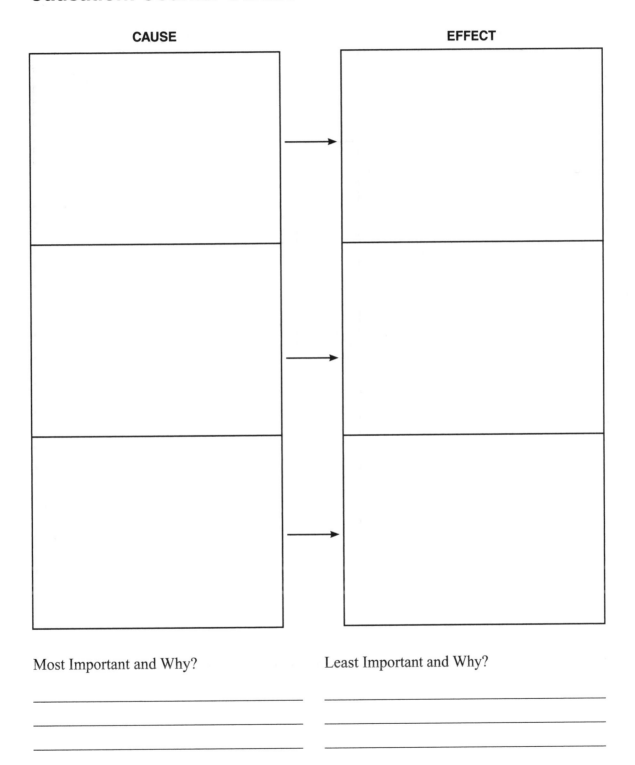

CAUSE   EFFECT

Most Important and Why?   Least Important and Why?

_____   _____
_____   _____
_____   _____
_____   _____
_____   _____

Causation: Rise of the New Right

CAUSE	EFFECT

Most Important and Why?

_____
_____
_____
_____
_____

Least Important and Why?

_____
_____
_____
_____
_____

Causation: New Economy of the 1990s

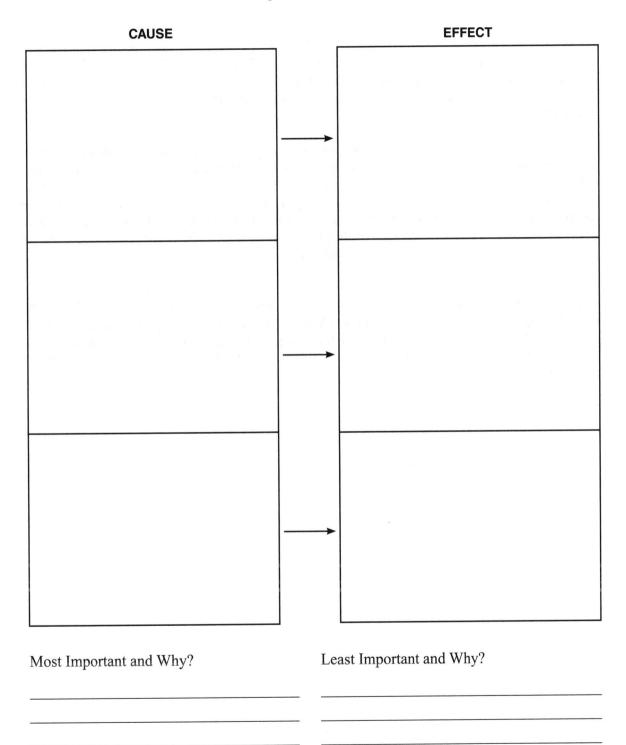

CAUSE   **EFFECT**

Most Important and Why?

_____
_____
_____
_____
_____

Least Important and Why?

_____
_____
_____
_____
_____

Student Instructions: Comparison

When we are asked to compare things, we are being asked to identify similarities and differences among the things under consideration. Similarities are the characteristics that they have in common, that is, the characteristics that are shared between the two things. Differences are the characteristics that are unique to any particular thing; in some cases, these characteristics can be contradictory to other characteristics.

The purpose of these Comparison graphic organizers is to analyze how similar and different certain historical topics are within their historical contexts. On the surface, it may appear that different topics have no similarities or differences; but upon further inspection, we often see that, indeed, many historical topics are more complex than we realized. But recognizing the similarities and differences is only the beginning of these graphic organizers' purpose. They ask us to dig deeper into our observations and to move from observation to evaluation. We should evaluate *why* there are similarities and differences between the two historical topics under observation.

The first graphic organizer in this category has been completed in order to serve as a model. In this sample, the two topics under investigation are the Federalists and the Democratic-Republicans. The sample demonstrates the different ways in which the two political parties might be compared. It is not important that you identify every detail of the topics' similarities and differences; instead, it is recommended that you come up with a few of the major ones, identify those on the Venn diagram, and be as specific and clear as possible.

Comparison: Federalists and Democratic-Republicans (1792–1824)

Political Democratic-Republicans
- Jefferson, Madison, Monroe primary of the state government
- Political support to France
- Opposed the Neutrality Proclamation

Economic Democratic-Republicans
- Agriculture and farming
- Supported the Louisiana Purchase
- Opposed a National Bank

Constitution defines and limits both the state and federal governments.

Belief in a strong economy; international power through trade and commerce

Political Federalists
- Washington, Hamilton, Adams primary of the federal government
- Political support to England
- Supported the Neutrality Proclamation

Economic Federalists
- Industry and manufacturing
- Hamilton financial program
- Supported a National Bank

Reasons for Differences:

Both groups had different groups of political support.

Different visions of Federalism

The balance between state and federal government

Reasons for Similarities:

Both groups took part in the Revolution at various levels and believed

strongly in the American cause.

Both groups believed in the weakness of the A.C. and that it needed revising.

Comparison: European and American Indian Cultures

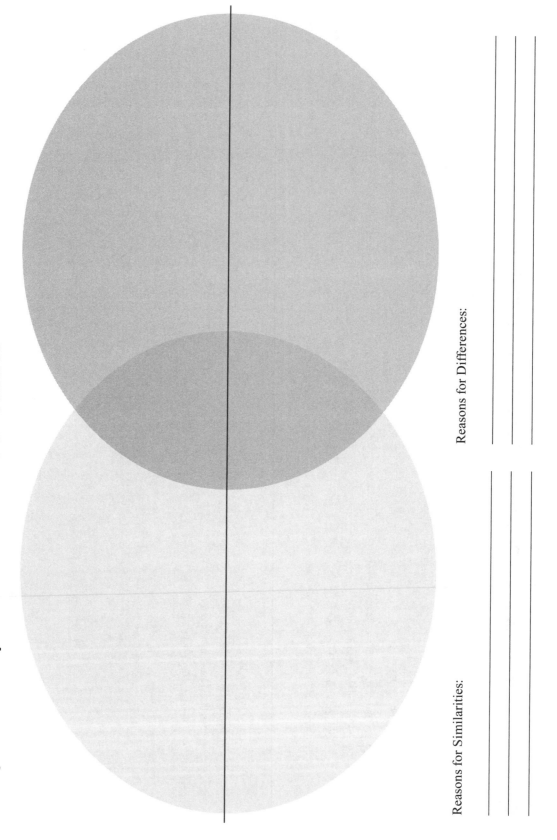

Reasons for Differences:

_____
_____
_____

Reasons for Similarities:

_____
_____
_____

Comparison: New England and Chesapeake

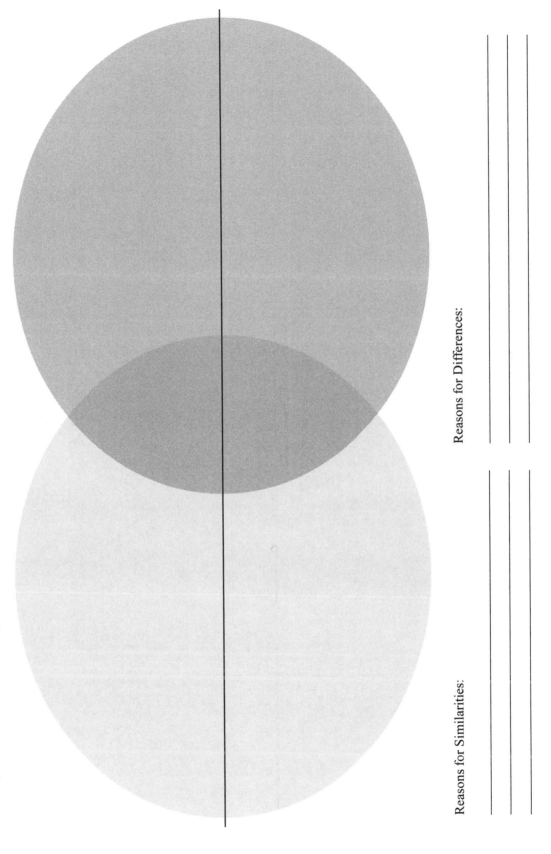

Reasons for Differences:
_____
_____
_____

Reasons for Similarities:
_____
_____
_____

Comparison: Indentured Servitude and African Slavery

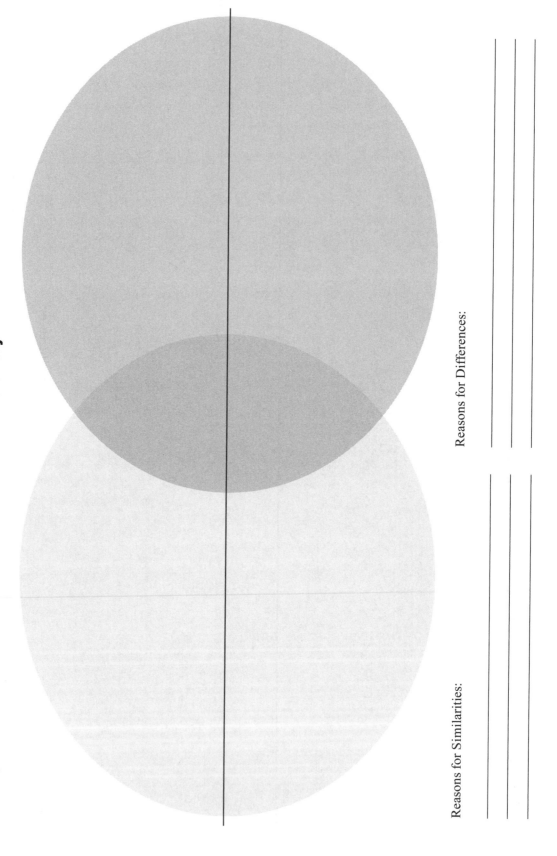

Reasons for Differences:

Reasons for Similarities:

Comparison: Loyalists and Patriots

Reasons for Differences:

Reasons for Similarities:

Comparison: Federalists and Antifederalists

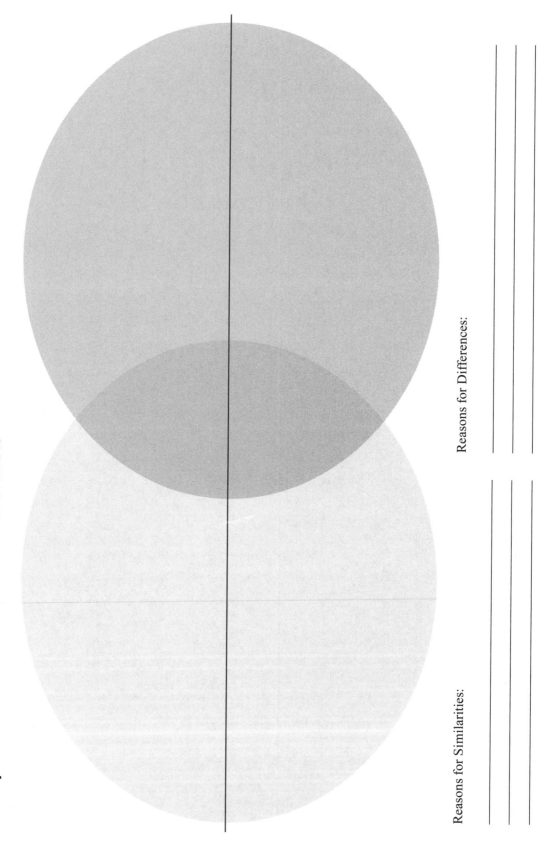

Reasons for Differences: _____
_____
_____

Reasons for Similarities: _____
_____
_____

Comparison: First and Second Great Awakening

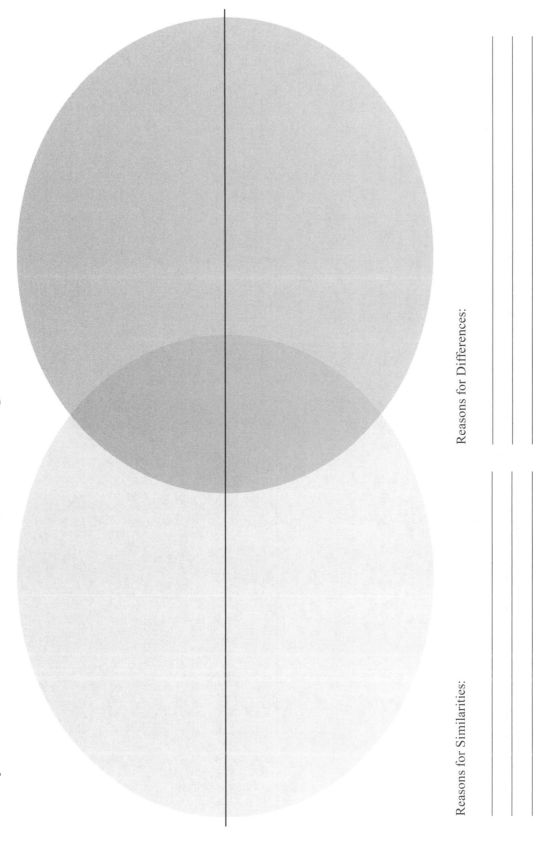

Reasons for Differences: _____

Reasons for Similarities: _____

Comparison: First and Second Wave Immigration (1620s & 1840s)

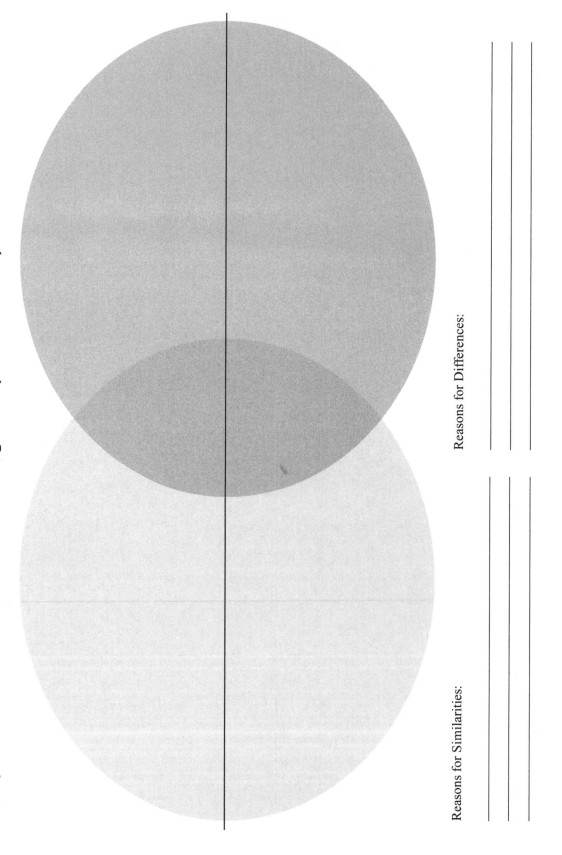

Reasons for Differences:

_____
_____
_____

Reasons for Similarities:

_____
_____
_____

Comparison: Whigs and Democrats (1828–1854)

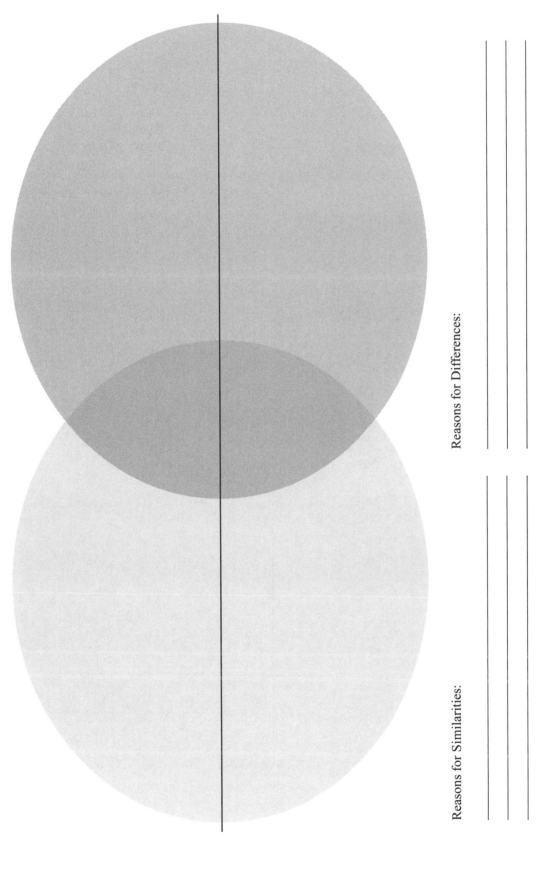

Reasons for Differences:

Reasons for Similarities:

Comparison: Upper and Lower South

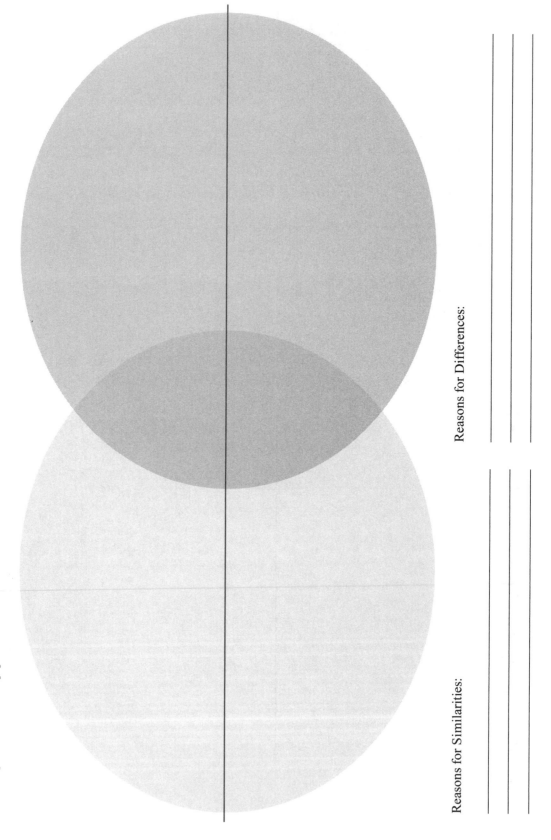

Reasons for Differences: _____

Reasons for Similarities: _____

Comparison: Moderate and Radical Abolitionism

Reasons for Differences: _____

_____

_____

Reasons for Similarities: _____

_____

_____

Comparison: North and South on the Eve of the Civil War

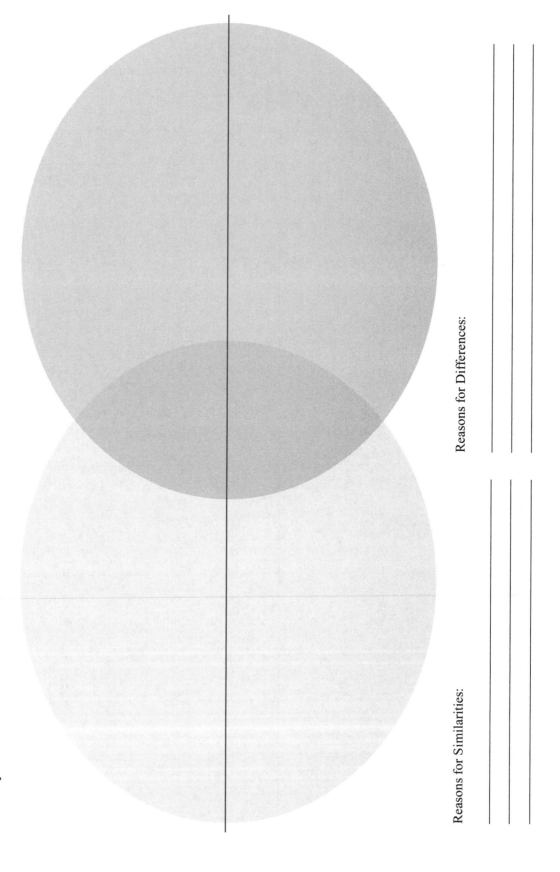

Reasons for Differences:

Reasons for Similarities:

■ NAME: _____

Comparison: Marshall and Taney

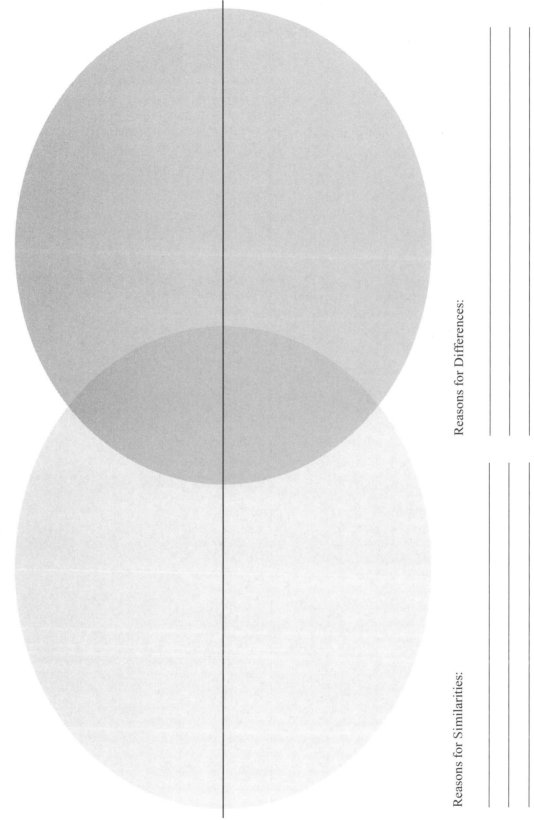

Reasons for Differences: _____

Reasons for Similarities: _____

CO13

Comparison: South before and after the Civil War

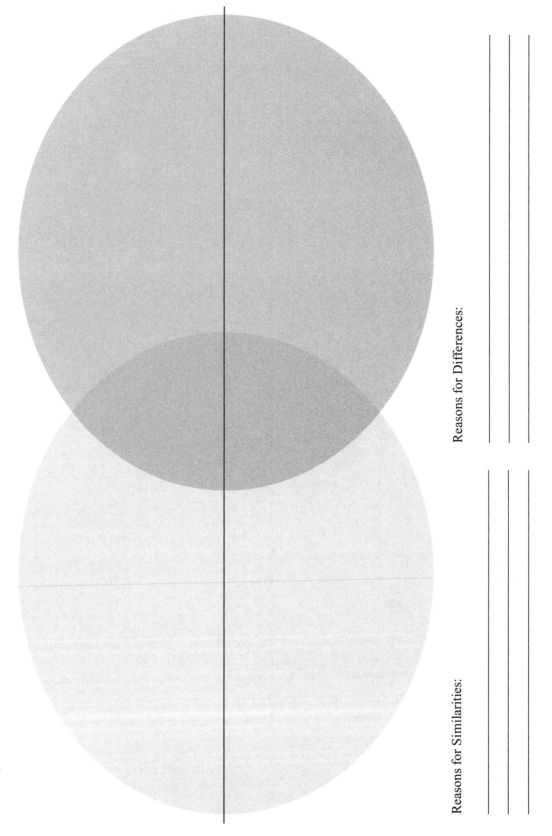

Reasons for Differences:

Reasons for Similarities:

Comparison: Market and Industrial Revolution

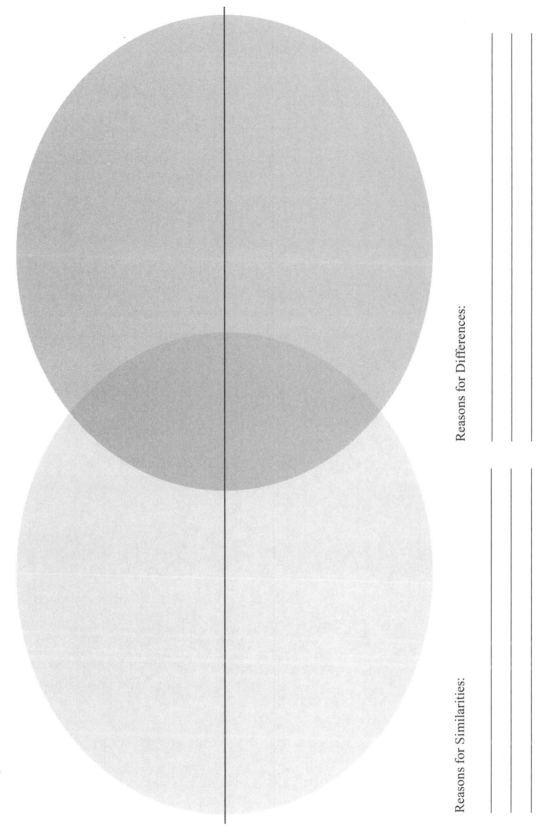

Reasons for Differences: _____

Reasons for Similarities: _____

Comparison: Democrats and Republicans (1854–1896)

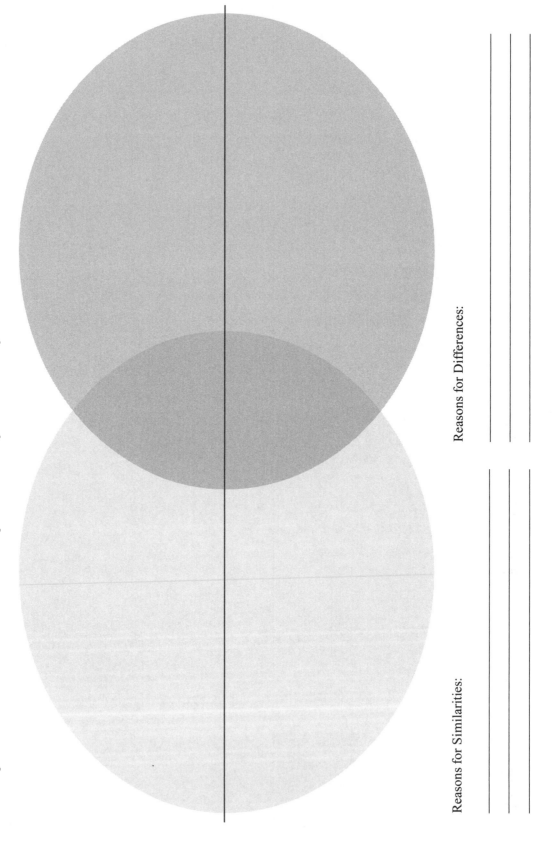

Reasons for Differences:

_____
_____
_____

Reasons for Similarities:

_____
_____
_____

Comparison: Second and Third Wave Immigration (1840s & 1880s)

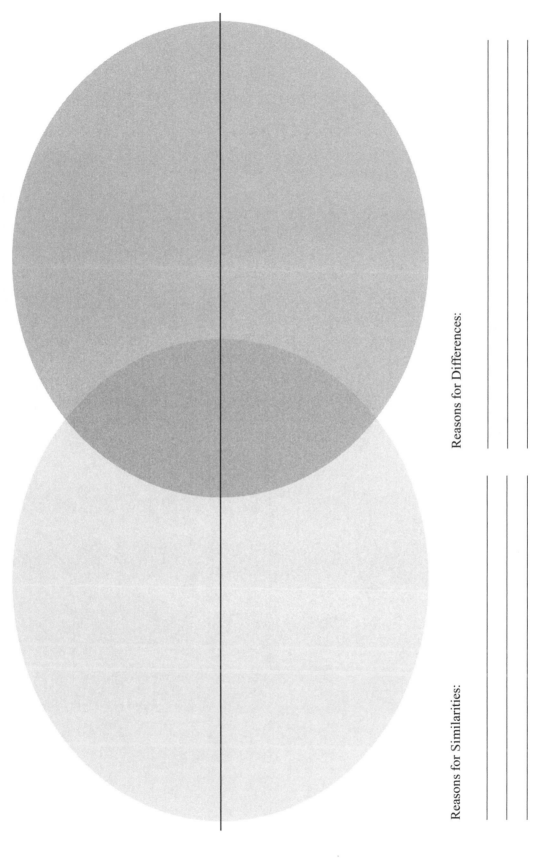

Reasons for Differences: _____

Reasons for Similarities: _____

Comparison: Manifest Destiny and Imperialism

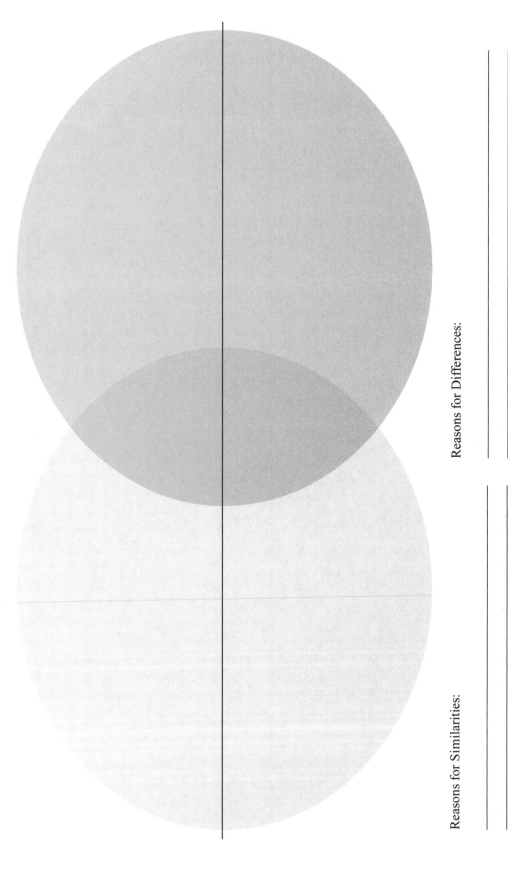

Reasons for Differences:

_____
_____
_____

Reasons for Similarities:

_____
_____
_____

Comparison: Social Darwinism, Gospel of Wealth, and Social Gospel

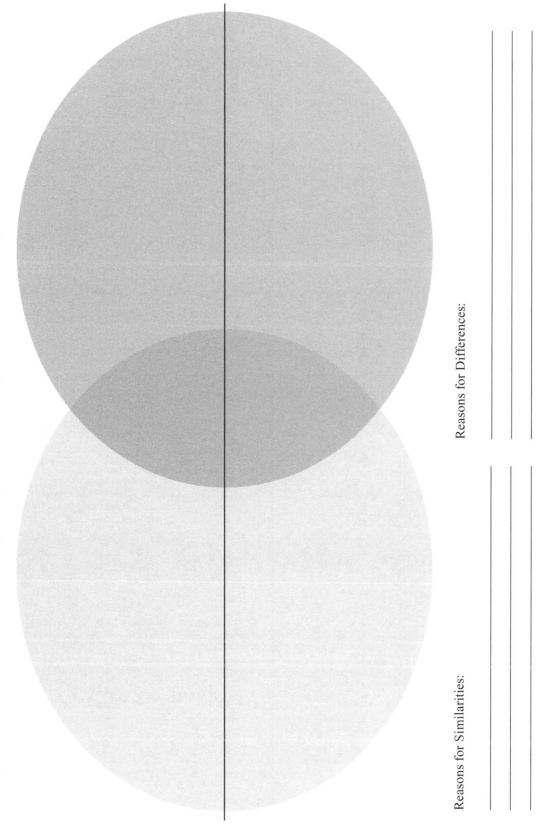

Reasons for Differences:

_____
_____
_____

Reasons for Similarities:

_____
_____
_____

Comparison: Populism and Progressivism

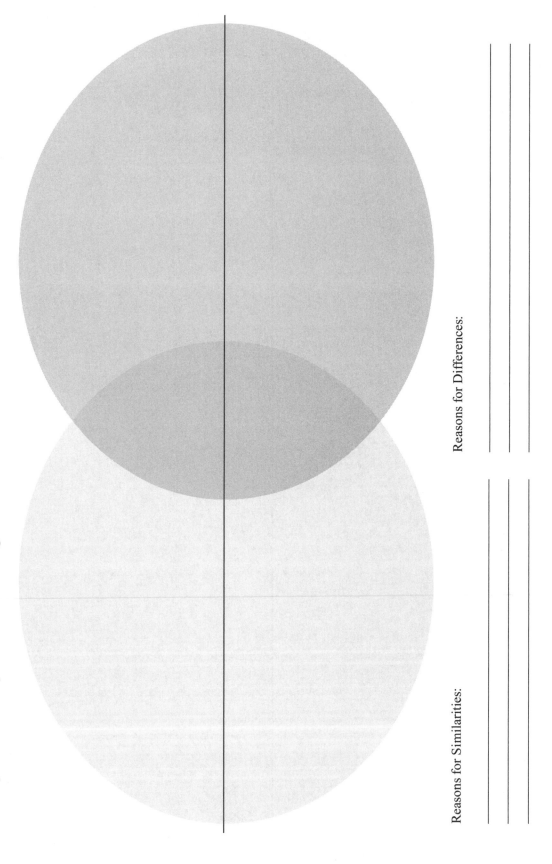

Reasons for Differences: _____

Reasons for Similarities: _____

Comparison: Roosevelt, Taft, and Wilson

Reasons for Differences:

_____
_____
_____

Reasons for Similarities:

_____
_____
_____

Comparison: Democrats and Republicans (1896–1932)

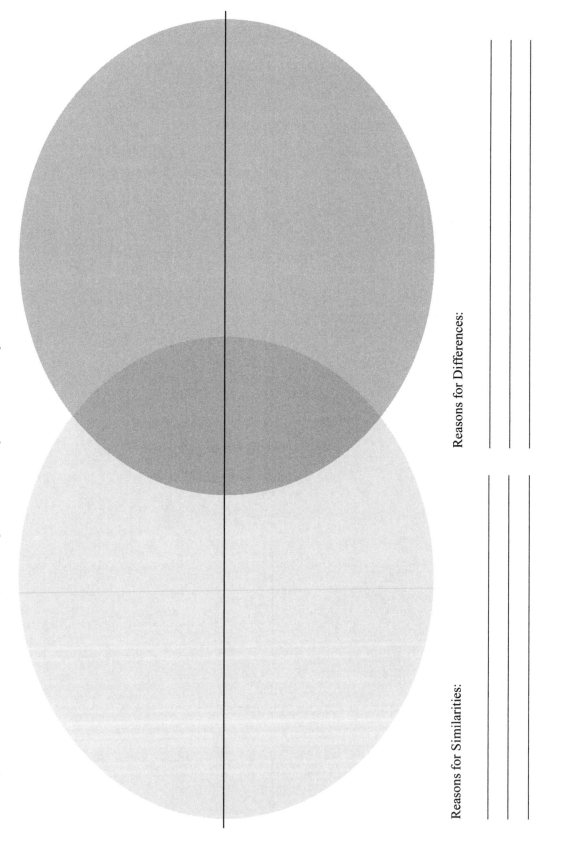

Reasons for Differences: _____

Reasons for Similarities: _____

Comparison: First and Second New Deal

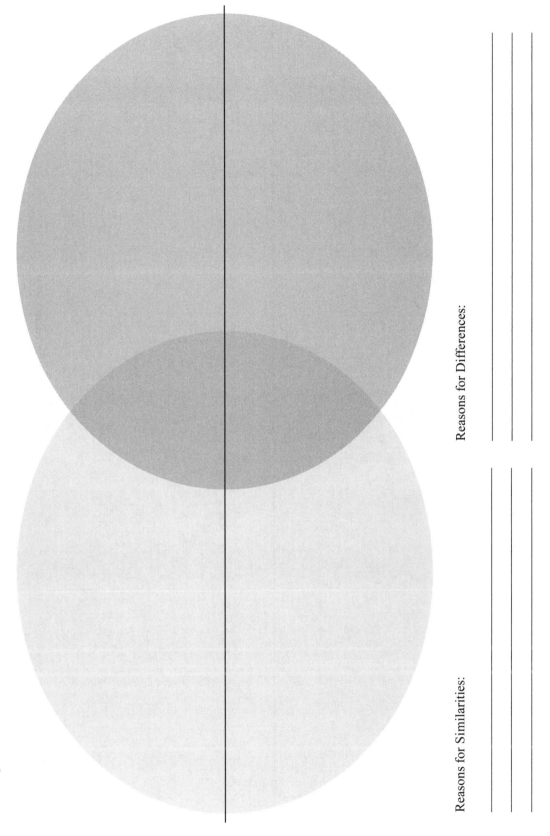

Reasons for Differences: _____

Reasons for Similarities: _____

Comparison: Women and Blacks during WWII

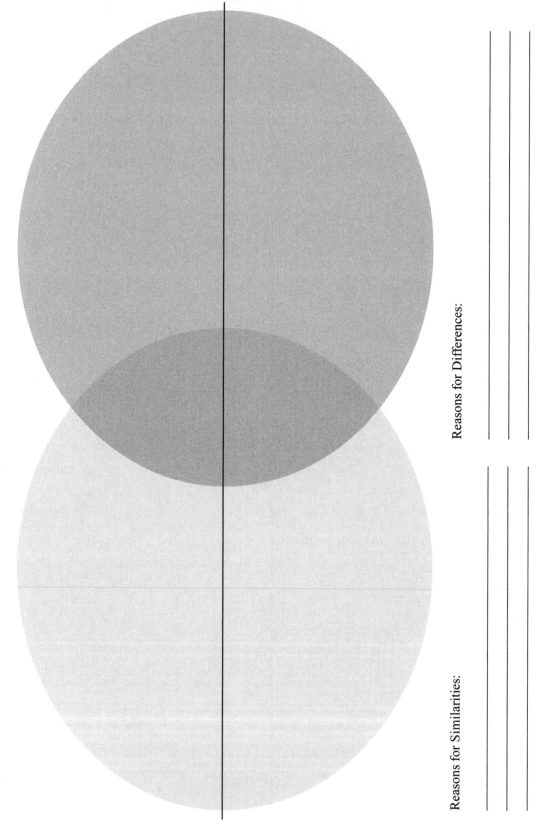

Reasons for Differences: _____

Reasons for Similarities: _____

Comparison: Home Front during WWI and WWII

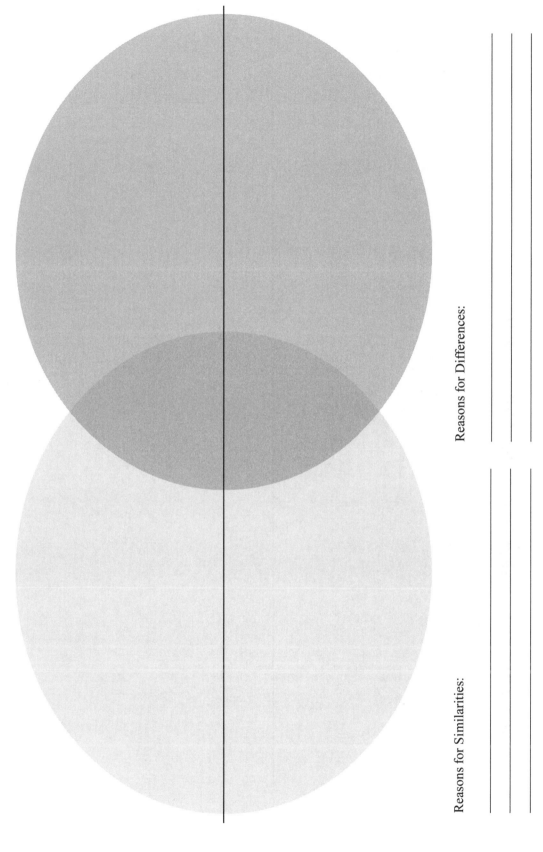

Reasons for Differences: _____

Reasons for Similarities: _____

Comparison: American Foreign Policy after WWI and WWII

Reasons for Differences:

_____

_____

_____

_____

Reasons for Similarities:

_____

_____

_____

Comparison: 1920s and 1950s

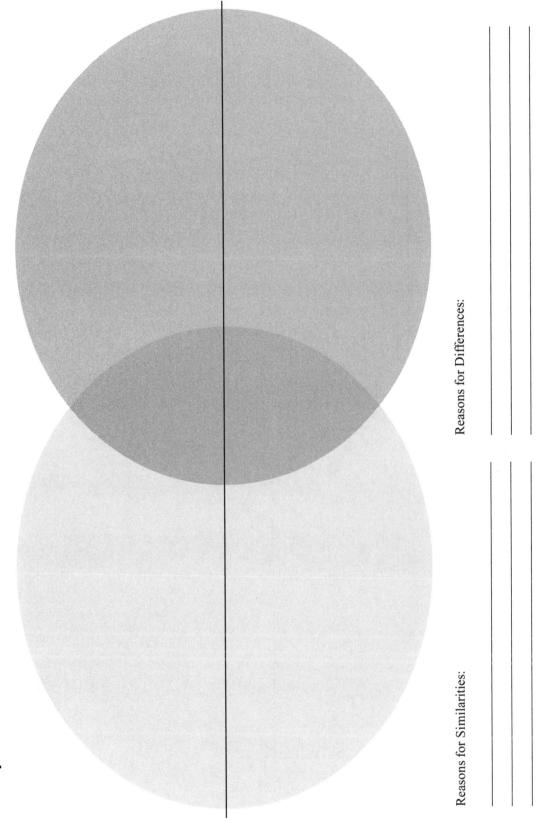

Reasons for Differences:

Reasons for Similarities:

Comparison: Malcolm X and Martin Luther King, Jr.

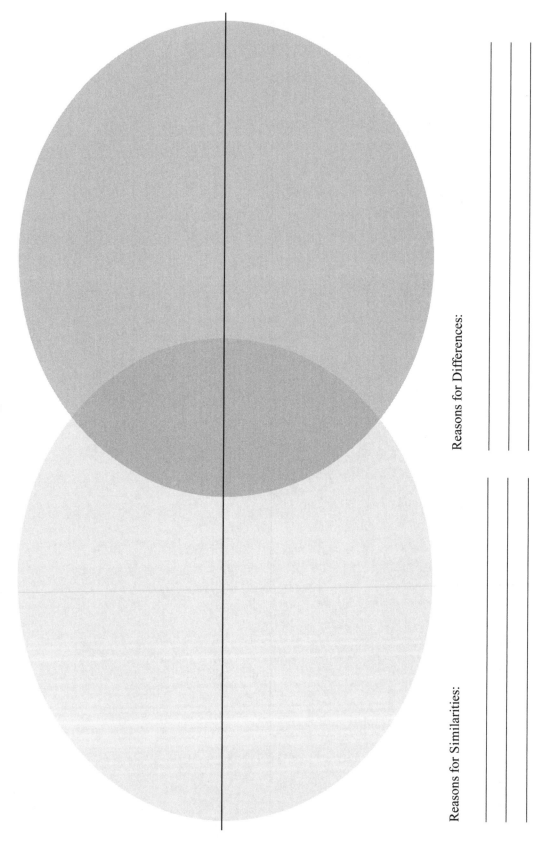

Reasons for Differences: _____

Reasons for Similarities: _____

Comparison: 1950s and 1980s

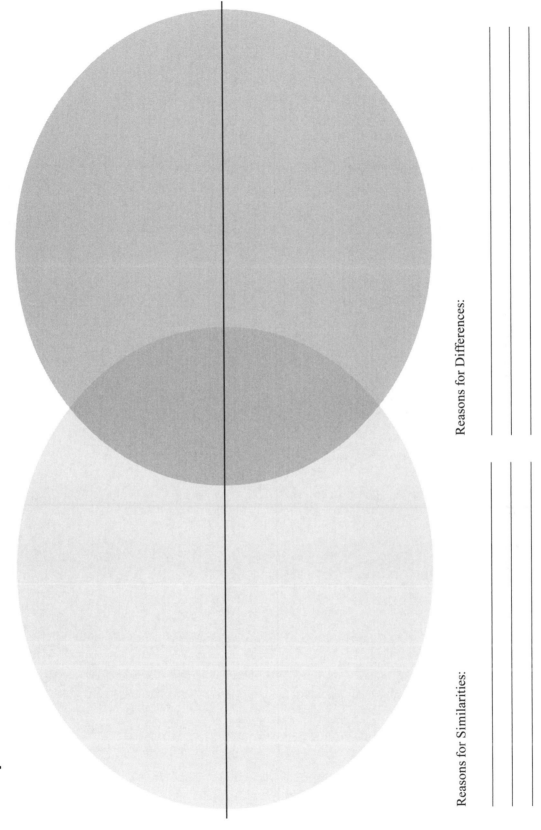

Reasons for Differences: ///

Reasons for Similarities: ///

Comparison: Democrats and Republicans (1933–Present)

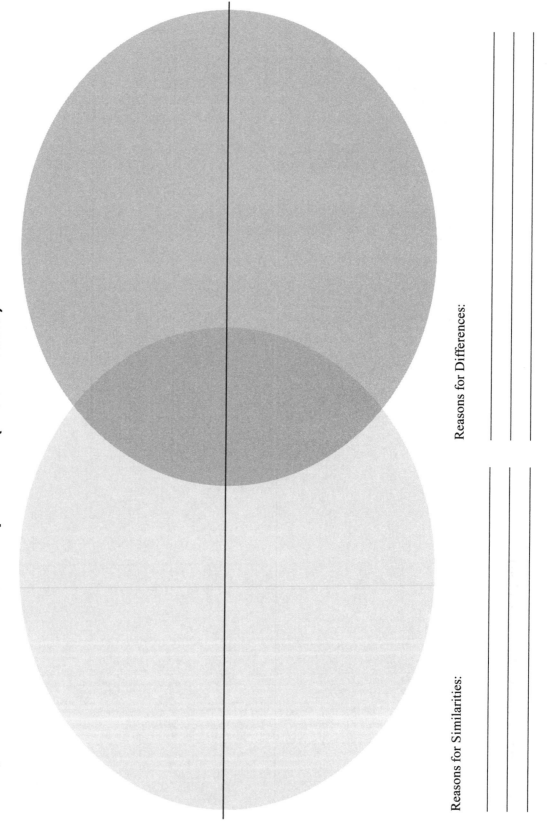

Reasons for Differences: _____

Reasons for Similarities: _____

Comparison: Counter Culture of the 1960s and Culture Wars of the 1990s

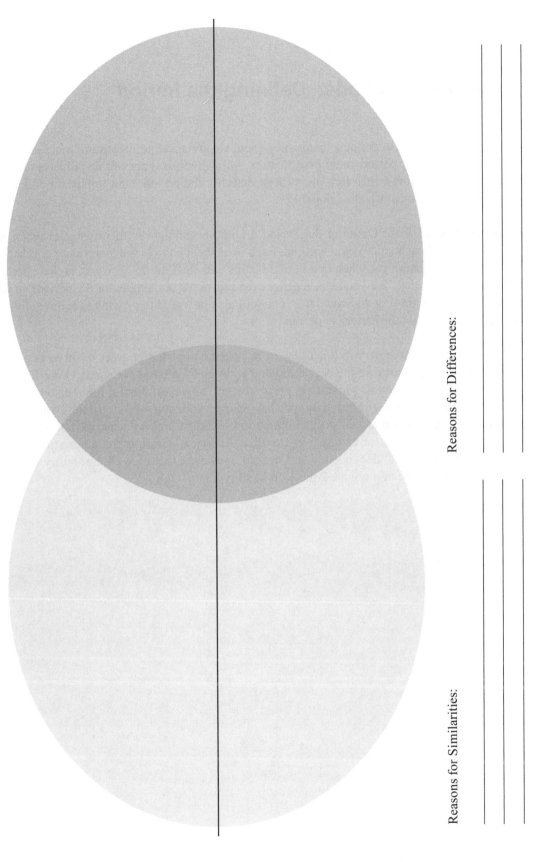

Reasons for Differences:

Reasons for Similarities:

Student Instructions: Defining the Period

When we are asked to define a historical period, we are asked to determine specific start and stop dates of events for the period under investigation. Many historical periods do not have clearly defined beginnings and endings; therefore, the task of defining the period is an important one and leads to much debate within historical scholarship.

The purpose of these Defining the Period graphic organizers is to investigate when important periods in American history begin and end. Each worksheet has a broad historical period about which you are asked to determine when that period begins and ends. In other words, is there some specific historical event or date that you believe defines the beginning and ending of the period? In addition to determining the beginning and end dates, you will also be asked to provide specific details that help define and contradict the historical period.

The first graphic organizer in this category has been completed in order to serve as a model. This sample worksheet focuses on the beginning and ending of Colonial America. There is probably less disagreement about when this historical period began; however, there might be some debate about when this historical period ended. After you have chosen your start and stop dates, you will first create a list of specific details that define this time period and then create a separate list of specific details that contradict them. So for example in Colonial America, defining characteristics might include things like the colonists' dependency on England. However, there are contradictory characteristics, such as the emergence of a unique American identity.

Defining the Period: Colonial Era

Start Date / Event: <u>1607</u>

Why?

Founding of Jamestown, first permanent English settlement in North America

_____

_____

End Date / Event: <u>1763</u>

Why?

End of the French and Indian War

_____

_____

DEFINING CHARACTERISTICS	CONTRADICTORY CHARACTERISTICS
• Colonists identify themselves as English. • Colonists have the same rights and privileges as English. • They see themselves as being distinct from Europe though. • Politically and financially the colonists are dependent on England.	• End of war changes the relationship. • End of war neglect • Beginning of taxes • Prior to the war there is an emergence of a unique American identity.

Defining the Period: European Exploration

Start Date / Event: _____

Why?

_____
_____
_____

End Date / Event: _____

Why?

_____
_____
_____

DEFINING CHARACTERISTICS	CONTRADICTORY CHARACTERISTICS

Defining the Period: American Enlightenment

Start Date / Event: _____

Why?

_____
_____
_____

End Date / Event: _____

Why?

_____
_____
_____

DEFINING CHARACTERISTICS	CONTRADICTORY CHARACTERISTICS

Defining the Period: American Revolution

Start Date / Event: _____

Why?

_____

_____

_____

End Date / Event: _____

Why?

_____

_____

_____

DEFINING CHARACTERISTICS	CONTRADICTORY CHARACTERISTICS

Defining the Period: Era of Good Feelings

Start Date / Event: ____

Why?

_____

_____

_____

End Date / Event: ____

Why?

_____

_____

_____

DEFINING CHARACTERISTICS	CONTRADICTORY CHARACTERISTICS

Defining the Period: Era of Nationalism

Start Date / Event: _____

Why?

_____

_____

_____

End Date / Event: _____

Why?

_____

_____

_____

DEFINING CHARACTERISTICS	**CONTRADICTORY CHARACTERISTICS**

Defining the Period: Era of Reform

Start Date / Event: _____

Why?

_____
_____
_____

End Date / Event: _____

Why?

_____
_____
_____

DEFINING CHARACTERISTICS	CONTRADICTORY CHARACTERISTICS

Defining the Period: American Renaissance

Start Date / Event: _____

Why?

_____

_____

_____

End Date / Event: _____

Why?

_____

_____

_____

DEFINING CHARACTERISTICS	CONTRADICTORY CHARACTERISTICS

Defining the Period: Secession Movement

Start Date / Event: _____

Why?

_____
_____
_____

End Date / Event: _____

Why?

_____
_____
_____

DEFINING CHARACTERISTICS	CONTRADICTORY CHARACTERISTICS

Defining the Period: Second American Revolution

Start Date / Event: _____

Why?

_____
_____
_____

End Date / Event: _____

Why?

_____
_____
_____

DEFINING CHARACTERISTICS	CONTRADICTORY CHARACTERISTICS

Defining the Period: Era of Reconstruction

Start Date / Event: _____

Why?

_____
_____
_____

End Date / Event: _____

Why?

_____
_____
_____

DEFINING CHARACTERISTICS	CONTRADICTORY CHARACTERISTICS

Defining the Period: Age of Imperialism

Start Date / Event: _____

Why?

_____

_____

_____

End Date / Event: _____

Why?

_____

_____

_____

DEFINING CHARACTERISTICS	CONTRADICTORY CHARACTERISTICS

Defining the Period: Progressive Era

Start Date / Event: _____

Why?

_____

_____

_____

End Date / Event: _____

Why?

_____

_____

_____

DEFINING CHARACTERISTICS	CONTRADICTORY CHARACTERISTICS

Defining the Period: Harlem Renaissance

Start Date / Event: _____

Why?

_____

_____

_____

End Date / Event: _____

Why?

_____

_____

_____

DEFINING CHARACTERISTICS	CONTRADICTORY CHARACTERISTICS

Defining the Period: New Deal Era

Start Date / Event: _____

Why?

_____
_____
_____

End Date / Event: _____

Why?

_____
_____
_____

DEFINING CHARACTERISTICS	CONTRADICTORY CHARACTERISTICS

Defining the Period: Cold War

Start Date / Event: _____

Why?

_____
_____
_____

End Date / Event: _____

Why?

_____
_____
_____

DEFINING CHARACTERISTICS	CONTRADICTORY CHARACTERISTICS

Defining the Period: Civil Rights Movement

Start Date / Event: _____

Why?

_____
_____
_____

End Date / Event: _____

Why?

_____
_____
_____

DEFINING CHARACTERISTICS	CONTRADICTORY CHARACTERISTICS

Defining the Period: Counter Culture

Start Date / Event: _____

Why?

_____

_____

_____

End Date / Event: _____

Why?

_____

_____

_____

DEFINING CHARACTERISTICS	CONTRADICTORY CHARACTERISTICS

Defining the Period: New Conservatism

Start Date / Event: _____

Why?

_____
_____
_____

End Date / Event: _____

Why?

_____
_____
_____

DEFINING CHARACTERISTICS	CONTRADICTORY CHARACTERISTICS

Defining the Period: War on Terror

Start Date / Event: _____

Why?

_____

_____

_____

End Date / Event: _____

Why?

_____

_____

_____

DEFINING CHARACTERISTICS	CONTRADICTORY CHARACTERISTICS

Student Instructions: Contextualization and Synthesis

When we are asked to consider contextualization and synthesis, we are being asked to first consider the historical setting of a particular event (i.e., the who, what, when, where, and why) and then to apply to that setting or context all the other historical thinking skills by drawing upon different subject areas as well as relevant (and even contradictory) evidence from primary and secondary sources.

The purpose of the Contextualization and Synthesis graphic organizers is to explore the different ways in which historians work with context. The first is what we call Local Context: the specific details that you can identify, which are closely connected to the event under investigation. The second is what we call Broad Context: the big picture. It is recommended that we think of the broad context in terms of connecting the topic under investigation to a major theme. The third is what we call Other Context: the connection of the topic under investigation to another period—"similar in kind, but at a different time." It also asks us to reflect on the circumstances surrounding the topic under investigation, then to think about another period (or geographic area) that has similar characteristics by looking forward or backward.

The first graphic organizer in this category has been completed in order to serve as a model. The specific event in this sample is the Declaration of Independence. The local context of this event could be that it was written primarily by Thomas Jefferson, it was signed in 1776, or it was approved by the Second Continental Congress. The broad context of "politics and power" was selected, so the specific details that follow help to explain how the event fits within this broad context or big picture. For the other context, a few specific details are provided to connect the two events, such as the Declaration of Independence to the French Revolution.

■ NAME: _____

Contextualization and Synthesis: Declaration of Independence

Circle one of the following themes:

American-National Identity   Work-Exchange-Technology   America in the World   Migration-Settlement   (Politics-Power)

Geography-Environment   Culture-Society

Explain the BROADER historical context (connect it to the theme chosen above):

Natural Rights, Lockean Social Contract Theory, Right to Self Government, Right to Revolution, End of French and Indian War leads to conflicts with British

officials about taxation, Representation in Parliament denied

---

Other Historical Context:
Forward Looking
South Carolina Declaration of Secession—
Southern Independence

Local Historical Context: (details)
South Carolina
1860
Southern Secession Conventions

↑

Declaration of Independence

Local Historical Context: (details)
Jefferson, Adams, Franklin
1776
Second Continental Congress
Philadelphia
"No taxation without representation"
Political representation

↓

Other Historical Context:
Backward Looking

Local Historical Context: (details)

Contextualization and Synthesis: First Great Migration

Circle one of the following themes:

American-National Identity   Work-Exchange-Technology   America in the World   Migration-Settlement   Politics-Power

Geography-Environment   Culture-Society

Explain the BROADER historical context (connect it to the theme chosen above):

Other Historical Context:

Local Historical Context: (details)

↑

First Great Migration

Local Historical Context: (details)

↓

Other Historical Context:

Local Historical Context: (details)

■ NAME: _____

Contextualization and Synthesis: Salem Witch Trials

Circle one of the following themes:

American-National Identity   Work-Exchange-Technology   America in the World   Migration-Settlement   Politics-Power

Geography-Environment   Culture-Society

Explain the BROADER historical context (connect it to the theme chosen above):

Salem Witch Trials

Other Historical Context:

Local Historical Context: (details)

Other Historical Context:

Local Historical Context: (details)

Local Historical Context: (details)

Local Historical Context: (details)

■ NAME: _____

Contextualization and Synthesis: Bacon's Rebellion

Circle one of the following themes:

American-National Identity   Work-Exchange-Technology   America in the World   Migration-Settlement   Politics-Power

Geography-Environment   Culture-Society

Explain the BROADER historical context (connect it to the theme chosen above):

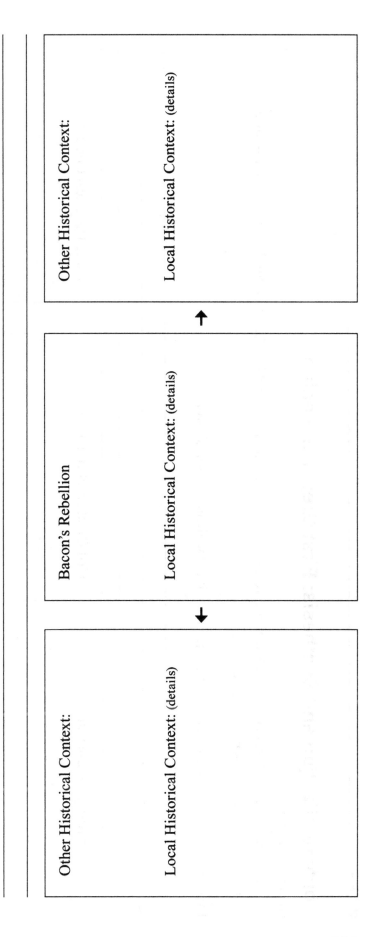

Other Historical Context:

Local Historical Context: (details)

Bacon's Rebellion

Local Historical Context: (details)

↑

↓

Other Historical Context:

Local Historical Context: (details)

Local Historical Context: (details)

■ NAME: _____

Contextualization and Synthesis: First Great Awakening

Circle one of the following themes:

American-National Identity   Work-Exchange-Technology   America in the World   Migration-Settlement   Politics-Power

Geography-Environment   Culture-Society

Explain the BROADER historical context (connect it to the theme chosen above): _____

Other Historical Context:	First Great Awakening	Other Historical Context:
Local Historical Context: (details)	Local Historical Context: (details)	Local Historical Context: (details)

Contextualization and Synthesis: Second Great Awakening

Circle one of the following themes:

American-National Identity   Work-Exchange-Technology   America in the World   Migration-Settlement   Politics-Power

Geography-Environment   Culture-Society

Explain the BROADER historical context (connect it to the theme chosen above):

Second Great Awakening
Local Historical Context: (details)

Other Historical Context:

Local Historical Context: (details)

Other Historical Context:

Local Historical Context: (details)

Contextualization and Synthesis: Republican Motherhood

Circle one of the following themes:

American-National Identity   Work-Exchange-Technology   America in the World   Migration-Settlement   Politics-Power

Geography-Environment   Culture-Society

Explain the BROADER historical context (connect it to the theme chosen above):

Other Historical Context:	Republican Motherhood	Other Historical Context:
Local Historical Context: (details)	Local Historical Context: (details)	Local Historical Context: (details)

Contextualization and Synthesis: Alien and Sedition Acts

Circle one of the following themes:

American-National Identity   Work-Exchange-Technology   America in the World   Migration-Settlement   Politics-Power

Geography-Environment   Culture-Society

Explain the BROADER historical context (connect it to the theme chosen above):

Other Historical Context:		Alien and Sedition Acts		Other Historical Context:
Local Historical Context: (details)	←	Local Historical Context: (details)	↑	Local Historical Context: (details)
		↓		
		Local Historical Context: (details)		

■ NAME: _____

Contextualization and Synthesis: American System

Circle one of the following themes:

American-National Identity   Work-Exchange-Technology   America in the World   Politics-Power

Geography-Environment   Culture-Society

Explain the BROADER historical context (connect it to the theme chosen above):

_____

Other Historical Context:

Local Historical Context: (details)

↑

American System

Local Historical Context: (details)

↓

Other Historical Context:

Local Historical Context: (details)

Other Historical Context:

Local Historical Context: (details)

Contextualization and Synthesis: Monroe Doctrine

Circle one of the following themes:

American-National Identity　Work-Exchange-Technology　America in the World　Migration-Settlement　Politics-Power

Geography-Environment　Culture-Society

Explain the BROADER historical context (connect it to the theme chosen above):

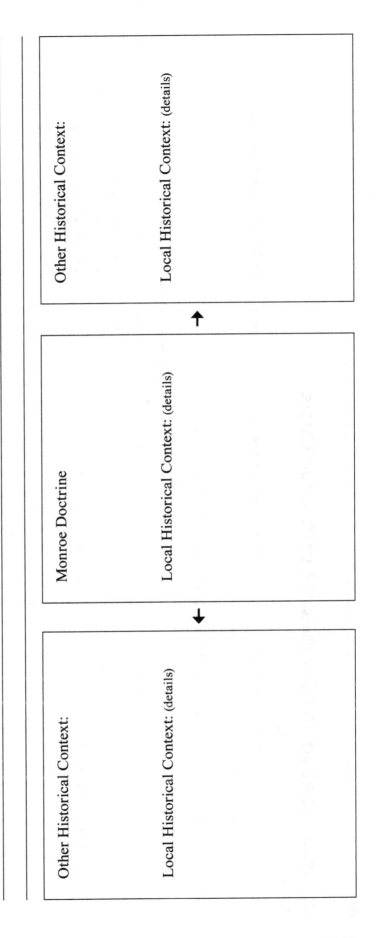

Other Historical Context:

Local Historical Context: (details)

Monroe Doctrine

Local Historical Context: (details)

Local Historical Context: (details)

Other Historical Context:

Local Historical Context: (details)

CS10

■ NAME: _____

Contextualization and Synthesis: Nullification Crisis

Circle one of the following themes:

American-National Identity   Work-Exchange-Technology   America in the World   Migration-Settlement   Politics-Power

Geography-Environment   Culture-Society

Explain the BROADER historical context (connect it to the theme chosen above):

Other Historical Context:	Nullification Crisis	Other Historical Context:
Local Historical Context: (details)	Local Historical Context: (details)	Local Historical Context: (details)

Contextualization and Synthesis: Missouri Compromise

Circle one of the following themes:

American-National Identity   Work-Exchange-Technology   America in the World   Migration-Settlement   Politics-Power

Geography-Environment   Culture-Society

Explain the BROADER historical context (connect it to the theme chosen above):

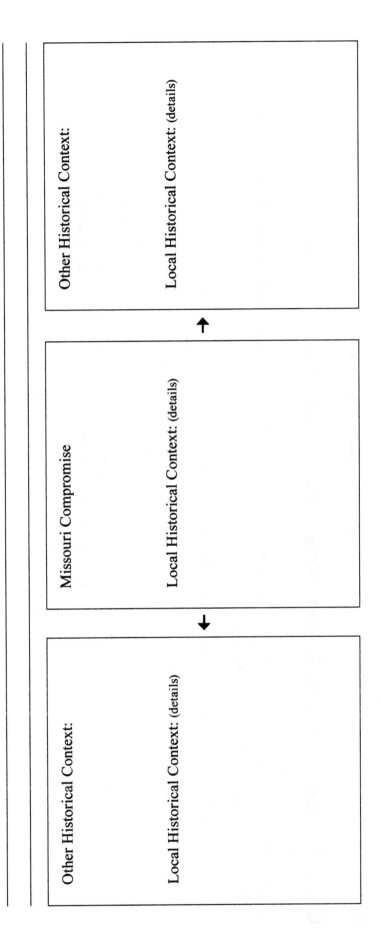

Other Historical Context:

Local Historical Context: (details)

Missouri Compromise

Local Historical Context: (details)

Other Historical Context:

Local Historical Context: (details)

Local Historical Context: (details)

Contextualization and Synthesis: Seneca Falls Convention

Circle one of the following themes:

American-National Identity   Work-Exchange-Technology   America in the World   Migration-Settlement   Politics-Power

Geography-Environment   Culture-Society

Explain the BROADER historical context (connect it to the theme chosen above):

Other Historical Context:	Seneca Falls Convention	Other Historical Context:
Local Historical Context: (details)	Local Historical Context: (details)	Local Historical Context: (details)

Contextualization and Synthesis: Annexation of Texas

Circle one of the following themes:

American-National Identity   Work-Exchange-Technology   America in the World   Migration-Settlement   Politics-Power

Geography-Environment   Culture-Society

Explain the BROADER historical context (connect it to the theme chosen above):

Other Historical Context:	Annexation of Texas	Other Historical Context:
Local Historical Context: (details)	Local Historical Context: (details)	Local Historical Context: (details)

Contextualization and Synthesis: Compromise of 1850

Circle one of the following themes:

American-National Identity   Work-Exchange-Technology   America in the World   Migration-Settlement   Politics-Power

Geography-Environment   Culture-Society

Explain the BROADER historical context (connect it to the theme chosen above):

_____

_____

Other Historical Context:

Local Historical Context: (details)

↓

Compromise of 1850

Local Historical Context: (details)

↑

Other Historical Context:

Local Historical Context: (details)

Contextualization and Synthesis: Wilmot Proviso

Circle one of the following themes:

American-National Identity   Work-Exchange-Technology   America in the World   Migration-Settlement   Politics-Power

Geography-Environment   Culture-Society

Explain the BROADER historical context (connect it to the theme chosen above):

Other Historical Context:		Other Historical Context:
Local Historical Context: (details)	Wilmot Proviso Local Historical Context: (details)	Local Historical Context: (details)
	↑	
Local Historical Context: (details)	↓	

Contextualization and Synthesis: Radical Republicans

Circle one of the following themes:

American-National Identity   Work-Exchange-Technology   America in the World   Migration-Settlement   Politics-Power

Geography-Environment   Culture-Society

Explain the BROADER historical context (connect it to the theme chosen above):

Other Historical Context:

Local Historical Context: (details)

Radical Republicans

Local Historical Context: (details)

Other Historical Context:

Local Historical Context: (details)

Contextualization and Synthesis: Muckrakers

Circle one of the following themes:

American-National Identity   Work-Exchange-Technology   America in the World   Migration-Settlement   Politics-Power

Geography-Environment   Culture-Society

Explain the BROADER historical context (connect it to the theme chosen above):

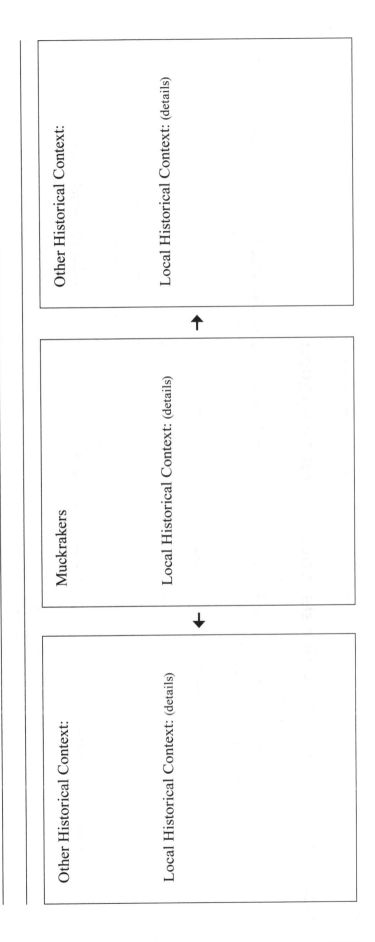

■ NAME: _____

Contextualization and Synthesis: Second Great Migration

Circle one of the following themes:

American-National Identity   Work-Exchange-Technology   America in the World   Migration-Settlement   Politics-Power

Geography-Environment   Culture-Society

Explain the BROADER historical context (connect it to the theme chosen above):

Other Historical Context: Local Historical Context: (details)	Second Great Migration Local Historical Context: (details)	Other Historical Context: Local Historical Context: (details)

Contextualization and Synthesis: New South

Circle one of the following themes:

American-National Identity Work-Exchange-Technology America in the World Migration-Settlement Politics-Power

Geography-Environment Culture-Society

Explain the BROADER historical context (connect it to the theme chosen above):

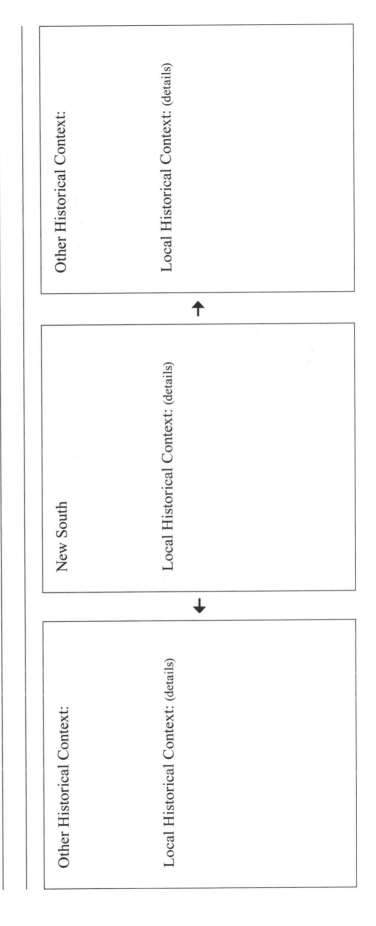

Other Historical Context:

Local Historical Context: (details)

New South

Local Historical Context: (details)

Other Historical Context:

Local Historical Context: (details)

Local Historical Context: (details)

■ NAME: _____

Contextualization and Synthesis: Red Scare of the 1920s

Circle one of the following themes:

American-National Identity   Work-Exchange-Technology   America in the World   Migration-Settlement   Politics-Power

Geography-Environment   Culture-Society

Explain the BROADER historical context (connect it to the theme chosen above):

Other Historical Context:	Red Scare of the 1920s	Other Historical Context:
Local Historical Context: (details)	Local Historical Context: (details)	Local Historical Context: (details)

Contextualization and Synthesis: National Recovery Administration

Circle one of the following themes:

American-National Identity   Work-Exchange-Technology   America in the World   Migration-Settlement   Politics-Power

Geography-Environment   Culture-Society

Explain the BROADER historical context (connect it to the theme chosen above):

Other Historical Context:	National Recovery Administration	Other Historical Context:
Local Historical Context: (details)	Local Historical Context: (details)	Local Historical Context: (details)

Local Historical Context: (details)

Contextualization and Synthesis: Four Freedoms

Circle one of the following themes:

American-National Identity   Work-Exchange-Technology   America in the World   Migration-Settlement   Politics-Power

Geography-Environment   Culture-Society

Explain the BROADER historical context (connect it to the theme chosen above):

Other Historical Context:

Local Historical Context: (details)

Four Freedoms

Local Historical Context: (details)

Other Historical Context:

Local Historical Context: (details)

Local Historical Context: (details)

Contextualization and Synthesis: Truman Doctrine

Circle one of the following themes:

American-National Identity   Work-Exchange-Technology   America in the World   Migration-Settlement   Politics-Power

Geography-Environment   Culture-Society

Explain the BROADER historical context (connect it to the theme chosen above):

Other Historical Context:	Truman Doctrine	Other Historical Context:
Local Historical Context: (details)	Local Historical Context: (details)	Local Historical Context: (details)

Contextualization and Synthesis: McCarthy Trials

Circle one of the following themes:

American-National Identity   Work-Exchange-Technology   America in the World   Migration-Settlement   Politics-Power

Geography-Environment   Culture-Society

Explain the BROADER historical context (connect it to the theme chosen above):

Other Historical Context:	Other Historical Context:
McCarthy Trials	
Local Historical Context: (details)	Local Historical Context: (details)

Local Historical Context: (details)

Local Historical Context: (details)

Contextualization and Synthesis: TV World

Circle one of the following themes:

American-National Identity   Work-Exchange-Technology   America in the World   Migration-Settlement   Politics-Power

Geography-Environment   Culture-Society

Explain the BROADER historical context (connect it to the theme chosen above):

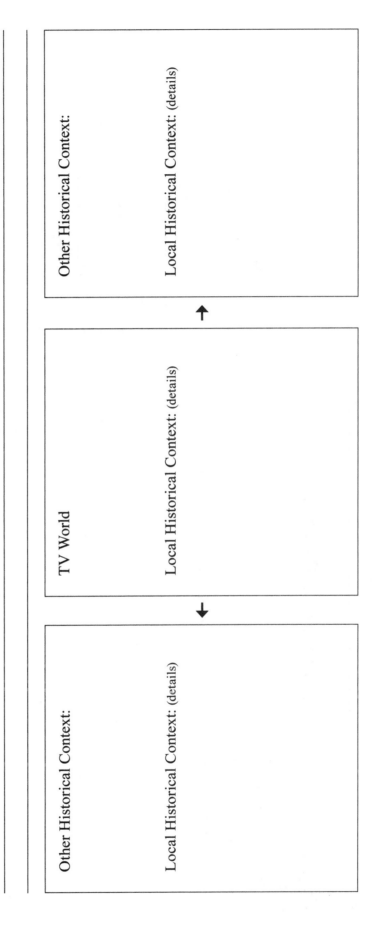

Other Historical Context:

Local Historical Context: (details)

TV World

Local Historical Context: (details)

Other Historical Context:

Local Historical Context: (details)

Other Historical Context:

Local Historical Context: (details)

■ NAME: _____

Contextualization and Synthesis: Détente

Circle one of the following themes:

American-National Identity   Work-Exchange-Technology   America in the World   Migration-Settlement   Politics-Power

Geography-Environment   Culture-Society

Explain the BROADER historical context (connect it to the theme chosen above):

Other Historical Context:	Détente	Other Historical Context:
Local Historical Context: (details)	Local Historical Context: (details)	Local Historical Context: (details)

Contextualization and Synthesis: Equal Rights Amendment

Circle one of the following themes:

American-National Identity   Work-Exchange-Technology   America in the World   Migration-Settlement   Politics-Power

Geography-Environment   Culture-Society

Explain the BROADER historical context (connect it to the theme chosen above):

Other Historical Context:	Equal Rights Amendment	Other Historical Context:
Local Historical Context: (details)	Local Historical Context: (details)	Local Historical Context: (details)

■ NAME: _____

Contextualization and Synthesis: Stagflation

Circle one of the following themes:

American-National Identity   Work-Exchange-Technology   America in the World   Migration-Settlement   Politics-Power

Geography-Environment   Culture-Society

Explain the BROADER historical context (connect it to the theme chosen above):

Other Historical Context:

Local Historical Context: (details)

Stagflation

Local Historical Context: (details)

↑

Other Historical Context:

Local Historical Context: (details)

↓

Local Historical Context: (details)

Contextualization and Synthesis: Reagan Revolution

Circle one of the following themes:

American-National Identity   Work-Exchange-Technology   America in the World   Migration-Settlement   Politics-Power

Geography-Environment   Culture-Society

Explain the BROADER historical context (connect it to the theme chosen above):

Other Historical Context:	Reagan Revolution	Other Historical Context:
Local Historical Context: (details)	Local Historical Context: (details)	Local Historical Context: (details)

Student Instructions: Turning Points

When we are asked to determine a turning point, we are being asked to determine how a single event brought about significant change in history. This is different from determining an event that brought about change over time, which normally requires us to consider multiple events and gives us a defined time period (e.g., How did the growing sectionalism lead to changes within American society from 1820 to 1860?). Determining a turning point focuses on a single event (e.g., How did the Kansas-Nebraska Act lead to the American Civil War?)

The purpose of these Turning Points graphic organizers is to explain the historical context of each of the three events and then determine which one of the events constitutes a turning point in American history. These graphic organizers prompt us to discuss what history was like before and after this particular event, helping us to confirm whether this event is, in fact, a turning point.

The first graphic organizer in this category has been completed in order to serve as a model. The three events under investigation are the Compromise of 1820, the Compromise of 1850, and the Election of 1860. The general topic of this particular set of events is the American Civil War. The sample first asks us to determine specific details of each of these three events, establish the historical context of each of them, detailing the who, what, when, where, and why of each event. Then, it asks us to select one of the events as the most important. In order to be able to articulate an argument for why you selected the event, it also will be important for you to articulate why you did not choose the other two. In other words, what is it about the event you selected that separates it from the other two? Why are the other two not your preferred choices, or less persuasive than the one you selected? Last, the sample asks us to provide some specific details as to what history was like both before and after the event.

Turning Points: Compromise of 1820 | Compromise of 1850 | Election of Lincoln

Give specific historical details (e.g., who, what, when, where, why) about these three events.

Compromise of 1820:

Also known as the Missouri Compromise

Admitted Missouri as slave state and Maine as a free state

Established the 36°30´ as the boundary

Compromise of 1850:

Result of the Mexican War

Admitted California as a free state; Utah and New Mexico decided by popular sovereignty

Tighter fugitive slave law

Election of Lincoln:

Abraham Lincoln elected as first Republican president.

Select one of the three events you believe to be a turning point in American history, then describe what it was like before and after that event.

America before the Election of Lincoln :

Compromise was possible.

Both North and South were willing to give up some ground.

Political parties had been around for awhile—similar visions.

America after the Election of Lincoln :

New vs. old guard

Compromise was no longer possible.

South Carolina votes to secede before election is official.

Civil War divides the nation.

Turning Points: Gutenberg Invents the Printing Press | Columbus's First Voyage to the New World | Martin Luther Launches Protestant Reformation

Give specific historical details (e.g., who, what, when, where, why) about these three events.

Gutenberg Invents the Printing Press:

_____
_____
_____
_____

Columbus's First Voyage to the New World:

_____
_____
_____
_____

Martin Luther Launches Protestant Reformation:

_____
_____
_____
_____

Select one of the three events you believe to be a turning point in American history, then describe what it was like before and after that event.

America before the _____:

_____
_____
_____
_____

America after the _____:

_____
_____
_____
_____

Turning Points: Establishment of Jamestown | Great Migration | English Civil War

Give specific historical details (e.g., who, what, when, where, why) about these three events.

Establishment of Jamestown:

_____
_____
_____
_____

Great Migration:

_____
_____
_____
_____

English Civil War:

_____
_____
_____
_____

Select one of the three events you believe to be a turning point in American history, then describe what it was like before and after that event.

America before the _____:

_____
_____
_____
_____

America after the _____:

_____
_____
_____
_____

Turning Points: First Navigation Act Passed | Bacon's Rebellion | Glorious Revolution

Give specific historical details (e.g., who, what, when, where, why) about these three events.

First Navigation Act Passed:

_____
_____
_____
_____

Bacon's Rebellion:

_____
_____
_____
_____

Glorious Revolution:

_____
_____
_____
_____

Select one of the three events you believe to be a turning point in American history, then describe what it was like before and after that event.

America before the _____:

_____
_____
_____
_____

America after the _____:

_____
_____
_____
_____

Turning Points: Proclamation of 1763 | Stamp Act Crisis | Battle of Lexington and Concord

Give specific historical details (e.g., who, what, when, where, why) about these three events.

Proclamation of 1763:

_____
_____
_____
_____

Stamp Act Crisis:

_____
_____
_____
_____

Battle of Lexington and Concord:

_____
_____
_____
_____

Select one of the three events you believe to be a turning point in American history, then describe what it was like before and after that event.

America before the _____:

_____
_____
_____
_____

America after the _____:

_____
_____
_____
_____

Turning Points: Articles of Confederation Ratified | Shays's Rebellion | Bill of Rights Ratified

Give specific historical details (e.g., who, what, when, where, why) about these three events.

Articles of Confederation Ratified:

_____
_____
_____
_____

Shays's Rebellion:

_____
_____
_____
_____

Bill of Rights Ratified:

_____
_____
_____
_____

Select one of the three events you believe to be a turning point in American history, then describe what it was like before and after that event.

America before the _____:

_____
_____
_____
_____

America after the _____:

_____
_____
_____
_____

Turning Points: Inauguration of Washington | Inauguration of Adams | Inauguration of Jefferson

Give specific historical details (e.g., who, what, when, where, why) about these three events.

Inauguration of Washington:

_____

_____

_____

_____

Inauguration of Adams:

_____

_____

_____

_____

Inauguration of Jefferson:

_____

_____

_____

_____

Select one of the three events you believe to be a turning point in American history, then describe what it was like before and after that event.

America before the _____:

_____

_____

_____

_____

America after the _____:

_____

_____

_____

_____

Turning Points: Election of 1816 | Election of 1824 | Election of 1828

Give specific historical details (e.g., who, what, when, where, why) about these three events.

Election of 1816:

_____

_____

_____

_____

Election of 1824:

_____

_____

_____

_____

Election of 1828:

_____

_____

_____

_____

Select one of the three events you believe to be a turning point in American history, then describe what it was like before and after that event.

America before the _____:

_____

_____

_____

America after the _____:

_____

_____

_____

_____

Turning Points: American Colonization Society Founded | Garrison's *The Liberator* | Stowe's *Uncle Tom's Cabin*

Give specific historical details (e.g., who, what, when, where, why) about these three events.

American Colonization Society Founded:

_____

_____

_____

_____

Garrison's *The Liberator*:

_____

_____

_____

_____

Stowe's *Uncle Tom's Cabin*:

_____

_____

_____

_____

Select one of the three events you believe to be a turning point in American history, then describe what it was like before and after that event.

America before the _____:

_____

_____

_____

_____

America after the _____:

_____

_____

_____

_____

Turning Points: Mexican-American War | Free-Soil Party Founded | John Brown's Raid on Harper's Ferry

Give specific historical details (e.g., who, what, when, where, why) about these three events.

Mexican-American War:

_____
_____
_____
_____

Free-Soil Party Founded:

_____
_____
_____
_____

John Brown's Raid on Harper's Ferry:

_____
_____
_____
_____

Select one of the three events you believe to be a turning point in American history, then describe what it was like before and after that event.

America before the _____:

_____
_____
_____
_____

America after the _____:

_____
_____
_____
_____

Turning Points: First Bull Run | Battle of Antietam | Battle of Vicksburg

Give specific historical details (e.g., who, what, when, where, why) about these three events.

First Bull Run:

_____

_____

_____

_____

Battle of Antietam:

_____

_____

_____

_____

Battle of Vicksburg:

_____

_____

_____

_____

Select one of the three events you believe to be a turning point in American history, then describe what it was like before and after that event.

America before the _____:

_____

_____

_____

_____

America after the _____:

_____

_____

_____

_____

Turning Points: Lincoln Assassinated | Radical Reconstruction Implemented | Compromise of 1877

Give specific historical details (e.g., who, what, when, where, why) about these three events.

Lincoln Assassinated:

_____
_____
_____
_____

Radical Reconstruction Implemented:

_____
_____
_____
_____

Compromise of 1877:

_____
_____
_____
_____

Select one of the three events you believe to be a turning point in American history, then describe what it was like before and after that event.

America before the _____:

_____
_____
_____
_____

America after the _____:

_____
_____
_____
_____

Turning Points: *Munn v. Illinois* | *Wabash v. Illinois* | *United States v. E. C. Knight Co.*

Give specific historical details (e.g., who, what, when, where, why) about these three events.

Munn v. Illinois:

_____

_____

_____

_____

Wabash v. Illinois:

_____

_____

_____

_____

United States v. E. C. Knight Co.:

_____

_____

_____

_____

Select one of the three events you believe to be a turning point in American history, then describe what it was like before and after that event.

America before the _____:

_____

_____

_____

_____

America after the _____:

_____

_____

_____

_____

Turning Points: Chinese Exclusion Act | *Plessy v. Ferguson* | Insular Cases

Give specific historical details (e.g., who, what, when, where, why) about these three events.

Chinese Exclusion Act:

_____

_____

_____

_____

Plessy v. Ferguson:

_____

_____

_____

_____

Insular Cases:

_____

_____

_____

_____

Select one of the three events you believe to be a turning point in American history, then describe what it was like before and after that event.

America before the _____:

_____

_____

_____

_____

America after the _____:

_____

_____

_____

_____

Turning Points: McKinley Assassinated | Upton Sinclair's *The Jungle* | Triangle Shirtwaist Fire

Give specific historical details (e.g., who, what, when, where, why) about these three events.

McKinley Assassinated:

_____
_____
_____
_____

Upton Sinclair's *The Jungle*:

_____
_____
_____
_____

Triangle Shirtwaist Fire:

_____
_____
_____
_____

Select one of the three events you believe to be a turning point in American history, then describe what it was like before and after that event.

America before the _____:

_____
_____
_____
_____

America after the _____:

_____
_____
_____
_____

Turning Points: Sherman Anti-Trust Act | Socialist Party Founded in America | Clayton Anti-Trust Act

Give specific historical details (e.g., who, what, when, where, why) about these three events.

Sherman Anti-Trust Act:

_____
_____
_____
_____

Socialist Party Founded in America:

_____
_____
_____
_____

Clayton Anti-Trust Act:

_____
_____
_____
_____

Select one of the three events you believe to be a turning point in American history, then describe what it was like before and after that event.

America before the _____:

_____
_____
_____
_____

America after the _____:

_____
_____
_____
_____

Turning Points: Assassination of Archduke Ferdinand | Sinking of the *Lusitania* | Zimmerman Note Intercepted

Give specific historical details (e.g., who, what, when, where, why) about these three events.

Assassination of Archduke Ferdinand:

_____

_____

_____

_____

Sinking of the *Lusitania*:

_____

_____

_____

_____

Zimmerman Note Intercepted:

_____

_____

_____

_____

Select one of the three events you believe to be a turning point in American history, then describe what it was like before and after that event.

America before the _____:

_____

_____

_____

_____

America after the _____:

_____

_____

_____

_____

Turning Points: Stock Market Crashes | Hawley-Smoot Tariff | Election of FDR

Give specific historical details (e.g., who, what, when, where, why) about these three events.

Stock Market Crashes:

_____

_____

_____

_____

Hawley-Smoot Tariff:

_____

_____

_____

_____

Election of FDR:

_____

_____

_____

_____

Select one of the three events you believe to be a turning point in American history, then describe what it was like before and after that event.

America before the _____:

_____

_____

_____

_____

America after the _____:

_____

_____

_____

_____

Turning Points: First Hundred Days Congress | American Liberty League Established | Supreme Court Declares New Deal Programs Unconstitutional

Give specific historical details (e.g., who, what, when, where, why) about these three events.

First Hundred Days Congress:

_____
_____
_____
_____

American Liberty League Established:

_____
_____
_____
_____

Supreme Court Declares New Deal Programs Unconstitutional:

_____
_____
_____
_____

Select one of the three events you believe to be a turning point in American history, then describe what it was like before and after that event.

America before the _____:

_____
_____
_____
_____

America after the _____:

_____
_____
_____
_____

Turning Points: Neutrality Acts Passed | Germany Invades Poland | Pearl Harbor Attacked

Give specific historical details (e.g., who, what, when, where, why) about these three events.

Neutrality Acts Passed:

_____
_____
_____
_____

Germany Invades Poland:

_____
_____
_____
_____

Pearl Harbor Attacked:

_____
_____
_____
_____

Select one of the three events you believe to be a turning point in American history, then describe what it was like before and after that event.

America before the _____:

_____
_____
_____
_____

America after the _____:

_____
_____
_____
_____

Turning Points: Yalta Conference | Marshall Plan | NATO Established

Give specific historical details (e.g., who, what, when, where, why) about these three events.

Yalta Conference:

_____
_____
_____
_____

Marshall Plan:

_____
_____
_____
_____

NATO Established:

_____
_____
_____
_____

Select one of the three events you believe to be a turning point in American history, then describe what it was like before and after that event.

America before the _____:

_____
_____
_____
_____

America after the _____:

_____
_____
_____
_____

Turning Points: Levittown Development Starts | *Brown v. Board of Education* | *Sputnik* Launched

Give specific historical details (e.g., who, what, when, where, why) about these three events.

Levittown Development Starts:

_____
_____
_____
_____

Brown v. Board of Education:

_____
_____
_____
_____

Sputnik Launched:

_____
_____
_____
_____

Select one of the three events you believe to be a turning point in American history, then describe what it was like before and after that event.

America before the _____:

_____
_____
_____
_____

America after the _____:

_____
_____
_____
_____

Turning Points: Greensboro Sit-Ins | March on Washington | Violence in 1968

Give specific historical details (e.g., who, what, when, where, why) about these three events.

Greensboro Sit-Ins:

_____

_____

_____

_____

March on Washington:

_____

_____

_____

_____

Violence in 1968:

_____

_____

_____

_____

Select one of the three events you believe to be a turning point in American history, then describe what it was like before and after that event.

America before the _____:

_____

_____

_____

_____

America after the _____:

_____

_____

_____

_____

Turning Points: Assassination of Kennedy | Gulf of Tonkin Resolution | Tet Offensive

Give specific historical details (e.g., who, what, when, where, why) about these three events.

Assassination of Kennedy:

_____
_____
_____
_____

Gulf of Tonkin Resolution:

_____
_____
_____
_____

Tet Offensive:

_____
_____
_____
_____

Select one of the three events you believe to be a turning point in American history, then describe what it was like before and after that event.

America before the _____:

_____
_____
_____
_____

America after the _____:

_____
_____
_____
_____

Turning Points: Reagan Elected | Glasnost and Perestroika | Dissolution of the Soviet Union

Give specific historical details (e.g., who, what, when, where, why) about these three events.

Reagan Elected:

_____

_____

_____

_____

Glasnost and Perestroika:

_____

_____

_____

_____

Dissolution of the Soviet Union:

_____

_____

_____

_____

Select one of the three events you believe to be a turning point in American history, then describe what it was like before and after that event.

America before the _____:

_____

_____

_____

_____

America after the _____:

_____

_____

_____

_____

Student Instructions: Continuity and Change over Time

When we are asked to identify continuity and change over time, we are being asked to identify a series of events over a distinct time period in history. Normally these events are centered on a specific theme with defined start and end dates within a period of American history.

The purpose of these Continuity and Change over Time graphic organizers is to investigate a series of events, place them in chronological order, then determine whether there was either more continuity or change during that historical period. When we are asked about continuity and change over time, there is almost always a significant change within the period under investigation. As with all of the graphic organizers in this book, there are no right or wrong answers. They will hopefully provide you with opportunities to articulate arguments for class discussions.

The first graphic organizer in this category has been completed in order to serve as a model. Notice that there are a variety of ways in which continuity and change over time can be investigated. For instance, in this sample, there is a timeline with clearly defined start and stop dates. Sometimes these dates will be specific, such as 1783 to 1856. 1783 was the end to the American Revolution with the signing of the peace treaty, and 1856 was the Kansas-Nebraska Act. Other timelines might have arbitrary start and stop dates; they may contain, for example, 1800 to 1850, which may represent specific events or may just represent a 50 year period. Try to provide 10 specific events for that time period. Once you have established a solid set of specific events, then identify three of the most important events for helping determine change or continuity. Identify these events, and then from that set, pick one as the critical event that led to a significant change within the historical period under investigation. From there you will need to identify what life was like before and after the event.

Continuity and Change over Time: Rise of Sectionalism in America from 1820–1861

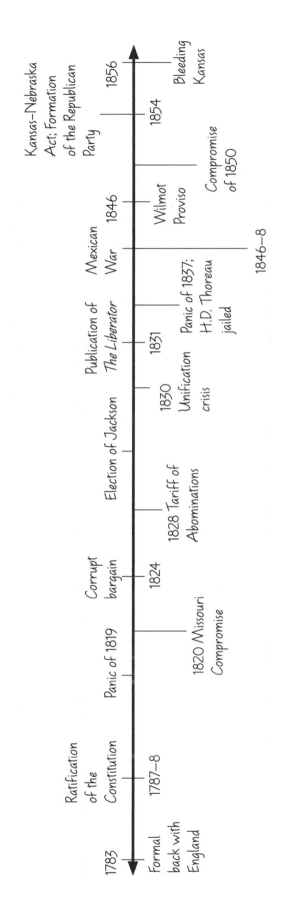

Timeline events:

1783 — Formal back with England

Ratification of the Constitution, 1787–8

Panic of 1819

1820 Missouri Compromise

Corrupt bargain, 1824

1828 Tariff of Abominations

Election of Jackson

1830 Unification crisis

Publication of The Liberator, 1831

Panic of 1837; H.D. Thoreau jailed

Mexican War, 1846

Wilmot Proviso

1846–8

Compromise of 1850

Kansas–Nebraska Act; Formation of the Republican Party, 1854

Bleeding Kansas, 1856

List three key dates / events from the timeline. Circle the most important one.

1820—Missouri Compromise   1850—Compromise of   1854—Kansas–Nebraska Act

Characteristics of the Country before: 1854

Both sides were willing to compromise

Territorial claims

Idea that popular sovereignty would determine slave issue

Civil war was not inevitable

Characteristics of the Country after: 1854

No longer willing to compromise

Kansas–Nebraska Act nullified the Missouri Compromise

Increasing violence was now deferring the issue over slavery

Civil war is inevitable

Continuity and Change over Time: America's Relationship with Britain from 1607–1776

List three key dates / events from the timeline. Circle the most important one.

Characteristics of the Country before: ____

Characteristics of the Country after: ____

Continuity and Change over Time: Religious Toleration in America from 1620–1786

List three key dates / events from the timeline. Circle the most important one.

Characteristics of the Country before: ____

Characteristics of the Country after: ____

Continuity and Change over Time: Development Democracy from 1776–1828

List three key dates / events from the timeline. Circle the most important one.

_____

Characteristics of the Country before: ____

_____
_____
_____

Characteristics of the Country after: ____

_____
_____
_____

Continuity and Change over Time: Role of Slavery in America from 1607–1855

List three key dates / events from the timeline. Circle the most important one.

_____   _____   _____

Characteristics of the Country before: ____

_____

_____

Characteristics of the Country after: ____

_____

_____

_____

_____

Continuity and Change over Time: Growth of Slavery in America from 1607–1865

List three key dates / events from the timeline. Circle the most important one.

Characteristics of the Country before: ____

Characteristics of the Country after: ____

Continuity and Change over Time: American Expansionism from 1800–1848

List three key dates / events from the timeline. Circle the most important one.

Characteristics of the Country before: ___

Characteristics of the Country after: ___

Continuity and Change over Time: Rights of Labor during the 18th and 19th Centuries

List three key dates / events from the timeline. Circle the most important one.

Characteristics of the Country before: _____

Characteristics of the Country after: _____

Continuity and Change over Time: Political Parties during the 19th Century

List three key dates / events from the timeline. Circle the most important one.

Characteristics of the Country before: _____

Characteristics of the Country after: _____

■ NAME: _____

Continuity and Change over Time: American Foreign Policy during the 19th Century

List three key dates / events from the timeline. Circle the most important one.

_____   _____   _____

Characteristics of the Country before: _____

Characteristics of the Country after: _____

Continuity and Change over Time: Role of Women in America from 1776–1860

List three key dates / events from the timeline. Circle the most important one.

_____   _____   _____

Characteristics of the Country before: ___

_____
_____
_____
_____

Characteristics of the Country after: ___

_____
_____
_____
_____

Continuity and Change over Time: Growth of America as an Economic Power from 1865–1900

List three key dates / events from the timeline. Circle the most important one.

Characteristics of the Country before: _____

Characteristics of the Country after: _____

Continuity and Change over Time: Relationship between the Government and the Economy from 1865–1940

List three key dates / events from the timeline. Circle the most important one.

_____   _____   _____

Characteristics of the Country before: _____   Characteristics of the Country after: _____

Continuity and Change over Time: Civil Rights Movement from 1948–1971

List three key dates / events from the timeline. Circle the most important one.

Characteristics of the Country before: ____

Characteristics of the Country after: ____

Continuity and Change over Time: Role of Women during the 20th Century

List three key dates / events from the timeline. Circle the most important one.

Characteristics of the Country before: ____

Characteristics of the Country after: ____

■ NAME: _____

Continuity and Change over Time: Political Parties during the 20th Century

List three key dates / events from the timeline. Circle the most important one.

_____

Characteristics of the Country before: _____

Characteristics of the Country after: _____

_____
_____
_____

Continuity and Change over Time: American Civil Liberties during the 20th Century

List three key dates / events from the timeline. Circle the most important one.

_____   _____   _____

Characteristics of the Country before: ___

Characteristics of the Country after: ___

Continuity and Change over Time: American Foreign Policy during the 20th Century

List three key dates / events from the timeline. Circle the most important one.

Characteristics of the Country before: _____

Characteristics of the Country after: _____

Continuity and Change over Time: Freedom of Religion during the 19th and 20th Centuries

List three key dates / events from the timeline. Circle the most important one.

_____

Characteristics of the Country before: _____

Characteristics of the Country after: _____

CT19

■ NAME: _____

Continuity and Change over Time: Rights of Labor during the 19th and 20th Centuries

List three key dates / events from the timeline. Circle the most important one.

_____ _____ _____

Characteristics of the Country before: _____

_____
_____
_____

Characteristics of the Country after: _____

_____
_____
_____
_____

Student Instructions: Argumentation

When we are asked to construct a historical argument, we are being asked to accumulate evidence and then to determine how it will be applied within the argument. The goal of historical argumentation is to convince an audience of the validity of our arguments.

The purpose of these Argumentation graphic organizers is to practice the necessary steps in constructing a valid argument. First, we must accumulate evidence that will support our arguments. Second, we must decide what evidence is compelling enough to side one way or the other on the topic at hand. Third, we must pick a side, and then begin the process of pre-writing. If we do not want to pick a side, we have the option of modifying the prompt—that is, agreeing and disagreeing simultaneously. Fourth, we need to establish our thesis statement. The thesis statement is a critical part of the argument. It's a road map for our audience: Where are you going and what routes are you going to take to get there?

The first graphic organizer in this category has been completed in order to serve as a model. Notice that, like all graphic organizers in this category, it has a specific prompt at the top of its page. It then asks us to determine specific data or details that would support or refute that prompt. *Support* means that we agree with the prompt and that we can support that prompt with specific details in a compelling way that would convince others that it is the correct assertion. *Refute* means that we disagree with the prompt and that we can refute that prompt with specific details in a compelling way that would convince others that is an incorrect assertion. *Modify* means that the prompt allows us to "sit on the fence," as it were. We can agree with the prompt in some ways, but then disagree with it in other ways—simultaneously agreeing and disagreeing. In the sample, we are asked to agree or disagree with the idea of Jefferson as being a strict interpreter of the Constitution. The first thing we should do is figure out how we want to organize the essay. This means coming up with two categories around which we want to organize our evidence. These categories can be based on social, political, or economic concepts or themes. (In the sample, they are "Pre-President" and "Post-President.) There is no right or wrong way to do this, but some categories will fit better than others. Next, we will need to construct a thesis statement. Once we have completed both of these activities, we have essentially written our essays.

Argumentation: "Thomas Jefferson maintained a strict interpretation of the U.S. Constitution."

Support, modify, or refute this statement with specific historical evidence.

SUPPORT (PRE-PRESIDENT)	REFUTE (POST-PRESIDENT)
Political	Political
• Promotes a strict interpretation • Opposes the bank; a political grandstanding (not defined) • Opposes Washington's Neutrality Proclamation (Congress has this authority, according to the Constitution)	• Supports the purchase of the Louisiana Purchase
Economic	Economic
• Opposes the creation of a national bank on economic grounds • Opposes Hamilton's financial plan	• Keeps all of Hamilton's economic plans in effect, except whiskey tax • Implements the economic embargo

Thesis Statement:

Jefferson, as Secretary of State under Washington, opposes many plans under the assumption that they are opposed to the U.S. Constitution, clearly identifying himself as a strict interpreter of the Constitution and thus a major opponent to Hamilton. However, as president, he changes direction and supports a number of economic plans of expansion and strong regulation of the economy. He also maintains the direction of the country under Washington. Therefore, he does maintain his philosophy as secretary of state, but somewhat reverses positions as president.

AR1

Argumentation: "European contact in the Americas sparked a positive change in the development of the Atlantic World."

Support, modify, or refute this statement with specific historical evidence.

SUPPORT	REFUTE

Thesis Statement:

_____
_____
_____
_____
_____
_____

Argumentation: "The founding of New England created a society of religious freedom and toleration."

Support, modify, or refute this statement with specific historical evidence.

SUPPORT	REFUTE

Thesis Statement:

_____

_____

_____

_____

_____

_____

Argumentation: "The American Colonies, prior to 1750, created a culture of opportunity and freedom very distinct from that in England."

Support, modify, or refute this statement with specific historical evidence.

SUPPORT	REFUTE

Thesis Statement:

_____
_____
_____
_____
_____
_____

Argumentation: "Bacon's Rebellion was a turning point in early Colonial America."

Support, modify, or refute this statement with specific historical evidence.

SUPPORT	REFUTE

Thesis Statement:

_____
_____
_____
_____
_____
_____

Argumentation: "The French and Indian War was a turning point between the Americans and the British."

Support, modify, or refute this statement with specific historical evidence.

SUPPORT	REFUTE

Thesis Statement:

_____
_____
_____
_____
_____
_____

Argumentation: "The American Revolution was the first attempt on the part of Americans to assert an American identity."

Support, modify, or refute this statement with specific historical evidence.

SUPPORT	REFUTE

Thesis Statement:

_____

_____

_____

_____

_____

_____

Argumentation: "The American Revolution created an environment that championed freedom and equality."

Support, modify, or refute this statement with specific historical evidence.

SUPPORT	REFUTE

Thesis Statement:

_____
_____
_____
_____
_____
_____

Argumentation: "Shays's Rebellion was a turning point for ratification of the Constitution."

Support, modify, or refute this statement with specific historical evidence.

SUPPORT	REFUTE

Thesis Statement:

_____

_____

_____

_____

_____

_____

AR9

Argumentation: "The Federalists articulated a much stronger vision for the country than the Antifederalists."

Support, modify, or refute this statement with specific historical evidence.

SUPPORT	REFUTE

Thesis Statement:

_____

_____

_____

_____

_____

Argumentation: "The Market Revolution was a turning point for the United States economic development."

Support, modify, or refute this statement with specific historical evidence.

SUPPORT	REFUTE

Thesis Statement:

_____

_____

_____

_____

_____

_____

AR11

Argumentation: "Slavery, as it developed in the United States, was unique from any other place in the world."

Support, modify, or refute this statement with specific historical evidence.

SUPPORT	REFUTE

Thesis Statement:

_____
_____
_____
_____
_____
_____

Argumentation: "Reform movements in the 19th century advanced democratic ideals."

Support, modify, or refute this statement with specific historical evidence.

SUPPORT	REFUTE

Thesis Statement:

_____
_____
_____
_____
_____
_____

Argumentation: "The Mexican-American War was a turning point for the institution of slavery in the United States."

Support, modify, or refute this statement with specific historical evidence.

SUPPORT	REFUTE

Thesis Statement:

_____
_____
_____
_____
_____
_____

Argumentation: "The Emancipation Proclamation was a turning point for African American freedom during the American Civil War."

Support, modify, or refute this statement with specific historical evidence.

SUPPORT	REFUTE

Thesis Statement:

_____

_____

_____

_____

_____

_____

AR15

Argumentation: "Republicans betrayed their roots by accepting the Compromise of 1877."

Support, modify, or refute this statement with specific historical evidence.

SUPPORT	REFUTE

Thesis Statement:

_____
_____
_____
_____
_____
_____

Argumentation: "The development of the West was a turning point in American history."

Support, modify, or refute this statement with specific historical evidence.

SUPPORT	REFUTE

Thesis Statement:

_____

_____

_____

_____

_____

_____

AR17

Argumentation: "The Spanish-American War was a turning point in American foreign policy."

Support, modify, or refute this statement with specific historical evidence.

SUPPORT	REFUTE

Thesis Statement:

_____
_____
_____
_____
_____
_____

Argumentation: "The Gilded Age was a period of economic prosperity and political equality for all Americans."

Support, modify, or refute this statement with specific historical evidence.

SUPPORT	REFUTE

Thesis Statement:

_____

_____

_____

_____

_____

_____

Argumentation: "America's involvement in WWI was an example, both at home and abroad, of 'making the world safe for democracy.'"

Support, modify, or refute this statement with specific historical evidence.

SUPPORT	REFUTE

Thesis Statement:

_____

_____

_____

_____

_____

_____

Argumentation: "The 19th Amendment was a turning point for women."

Support, modify, or refute this statement with specific historical evidence.

SUPPORT	REFUTE

Thesis Statement:

_____

_____

_____

_____

_____

_____

Argumentation: "The shift in population from rural to urban drove all the cultural clashes during the 1920s."

Support, modify, or refute this statement with specific historical evidence.

SUPPORT	REFUTE

Thesis Statement:

_____

_____

_____

_____

_____

_____

Argumentation: "The New Deal benefited all Americans during the Great Depression."

Support, modify, or refute this statement with specific historical evidence.

SUPPORT	REFUTE

Thesis Statement:

_____

_____

_____

_____

_____

_____

Argumentation: "WWII was a turning point for American foreign policy."

Support, modify, or refute this statement with specific historical evidence.

SUPPORT	REFUTE

Thesis Statement:

_____

_____

_____

_____

_____

_____

Argumentation: "The Truman presidency was a turning point for African Americans."

Support, modify, or refute this statement with specific historical evidence.

SUPPORT	REFUTE

Thesis Statement:

_____
_____
_____
_____
_____
_____

Argumentation: "NCS-68 was a critical document in positively defining America's role in the Cold War."

Support, modify, or refute this statement with specific historical evidence.

SUPPORT	REFUTE

Thesis Statement:

_____

_____

_____

_____

_____

_____

Argumentation: "*Brown v. Board of Education* was a turning point for African Americans."

Support, modify, or refute this statement with specific historical evidence.

SUPPORT	REFUTE

Thesis Statement:

_____

_____

_____

_____

_____

_____

AR27

Argumentation: "Johnson's presidency was a turning point for the civil rights movement."

Support, modify, or refute this statement with specific historical evidence.

SUPPORT	REFUTE

Thesis Statement:

_____
_____
_____
_____
_____
_____

Argumentation: "Nixon's domestic and foreign policies reflected a conservative agenda."

Support, modify, or refute this statement with specific historical evidence.

SUPPORT	REFUTE

Thesis Statement:

_____
_____
_____
_____
_____
_____

Argumentation: "The election of Ronald Reagan was a turning point for conservatives in the United States."

Support, modify, or refute this statement with specific historical evidence.

SUPPORT	REFUTE

Thesis Statement:

_____
_____
_____
_____
_____
_____

Argumentation: "Clinton's presidency ushered in New World Order."

Support, modify, or refute this statement with specific historical evidence.

SUPPORT	REFUTE

Thesis Statement:

_____

_____

_____

_____

_____

_____

Student Instructions: Interpretation

When we are asked to make historical interpretations, we are being asked to interpret excerpts from secondary sources. The difference between primary and secondary sources is the nature of when the excerpts were written. Primary sources are written by the historical figures under investigation (e.g., the Declaration of Independence is a primary source because it was written in 1776 by Thomas Jefferson). Secondary sources are written by historians about the historical figures under investigation (e.g., Carl Becker wrote *The Declaration of Independence: A Study in the History of Political Ideas* in 1942). Sometimes secondary sources can become primary sources, if the nature of the writing becomes so important that it lasts well into the future. Historical interpretation can involve either primary or secondary sources, but for the purposes of these activities, we will strictly stick to secondary sources.

The purpose of these Interpretation graphic organizers is to practice reading a variety of small secondary excerpts from important historical scholarship, which is a challenging task. Historians are often products of their environments, thus the language can serve as a deterrent to the reader. If the language employs terms that are no longer part of the vernacular, then the meaning can be lost. Another reason this can be a challenging task is because historians often agree on something, but disagree with regard to the importance of the event under investigation. For example, two historians may agree that the New Deal was bad for the country, but they may disagree as to why it was bad. One may argue that it was bad because it economically created a permanent group of citizens that rely on the government. Another may argue that it was bad because it fundamentally changed the political role of the government. Since this is one of the primary purposes of historiography—that is, the interpretation of historical events—it is important that we effectively engage secondary sources and interpret their different arguments.

The first graphic organizer in this category has been completed in order to serve as a model. Like every graphic organizer in this category, it has two secondary-source excerpts. Each excerpt pertains to a particular historical event, such as the "Causes of the American Revolution." They ask us to complete three tasks. First, determine the differences between the two authors. This should not be a restatement of the two excerpts. Instead, we must articulate each author's argument in our own words. Second, provide specific evidence, which is not specifically mentioned in the excerpt, supporting the first author. This will demonstrate a solid understanding of the excerpt. Third, provide specific evidence, which is not specifically mentioned in the excerpt, supporting the second author. This will demonstrate a solid understanding of the other excerpt.

Interpretation: Causes of the American Revolution

A: Not human stupidity, not dreams of new splendor for the empire, not a growing dissimilarity of psychological attitudes, but economic breakdown in the Mercantile System: the inability of both English mercantile capitalism and colonial mercantile and planter capitalism to operate within a contracting sphere in which clashes of interest were becoming sharper and sharper: this was the basic reason for the onset of crisis and the outbreak of revolutionary struggle. The mother country had bound the colonies to itself in an economic vassalage: opportunities for colonial enterprise were possible only in commercial agriculture and in trade. But when the expanding commercial activities of northern merchant capitalists came into conflict with the great capitalist interest of [the] British. . .then repression, coercion, even the violence of economic extinction had to follow. —Louis M. Hacker, *The Triumph of American Capitalism,* 1940

B: The Declaration of Independence was taken seriously by many Americans, or at least they found its basic philosophy useful in battling for change in the new states...by 1776 there were people in America demanding the establishment of democratic state governments, by which they meant legislatures controlled by a majority of voters, and with none of the checks upon their actions such as had existed in the colonies...The history of the writing of the first state constitutions is to a large extent the history of the conflict between these two ideals of government...The significant thing is...the alteration of the balance of power within the structure, and in the political situation resulting from the break away from the supervising power of a central government—that of Great Britain. —Merrill Jensen, "Democracy and the American Revolution," 1957

Explain the differences between Interpretation **A** and Interpretation **B**:

Hacker says that the developing economic situation, particularly the new economic opportunities that arose as a result of America's situation caused frustration on part of the British, leading to the revolution. Jensen says that it was more about politics and the growing desire for political participation within the colonies that began the road toward revolution.

Specific Historical Evidence to Support **A** (not mentioned in passage):

Passage of the Sugar Act was designed to limit and restrict trade of the American colonies. British merchants were angered over the economic opportunities of the Americas, they sought to limit trade, therefore limiting economic opportunities and freedom, to only with the British.

Specific Historical Evidence to Support **B** (not mentioned in passage):

The emergence of the Regulator Movement in North Carolina and South Carolina demonstrated the frustration of the Americans at getting land and representation in government. In South Carolina, it was about access to local government, but in North Carolina it was about access to land.

Interpretation: Assessment of Columbus

A: The Columbian discovery was of greater magnitude than any other discovery or invention in human history. Europeans realized that in the sixteenth century. In the centuries since then, the importance of Columbus's discovery has continued to swell, both because of the prodigious development of the New World and because of the numerous other discoveries that have stemmed from it. It was after Columbus's voyages that the task of integrating the American continents into Greco-Roman-Christian-European-culture was carried out. Notwithstanding errors, egoism, and unheard-of violence, the discovery was an essential, in many ways, determining, factor in ushering in the modern age. It was brought about first and above all by the Spanish and then by the Portuguese, French, English, Italians, Irish—to some extent by all the peoples of Europe. But this recognition cannot diminish the value of the inception of that task, which was Columbus's discovery.—Paolo Emilio Taviani, *Columbus, The Great Adventure*, 1991

B: Thus began the history, five hundred years ago, of the European invasion of the Indian settlements of the Americas . . . When we read the history books given to children in the United States, it all starts with heroic adventure—there is no bloodshed—and Columbus Day is a celebration. To emphasize the heroism of Columbus and his successors as navigators and discoverers, and to deemphasize their genocide, is not a technical necessity but an ideological choice. It serves—unwittingly—to justify what was done. . . . The treatment of heroes (Columbus) and their victims (the Arawaks)—the quiet acceptance of conquest and murder in the name of progress—is only one aspect of a certain approach to history, in which the past is told from the point of view of government, conquerors, diplomats, leaders . . . Was all this bloodshed and deceit—from Columbus to Cortes, Pizarro, the Puritans—a necessity for the human race to progress from savagery to civilization?—Howard Zinn, *A People's History of the United States*, 1980

Explain the differences between Interpretation **A** and Interpretation **B**:

_____

_____

_____

_____

_____

Specific Historical Evidence to Support **A** (not mentioned in passage):

_____

_____

_____

Specific Historical Evidence to Support **B** (not mentioned in passage):

_____

_____

_____

Interpretation: Pueblo Revolt

A: The fighting of 1680 caught the Spanish by surprise, and their evacuation left the Indians free to follow pre-contact standards of conduct as they wished. There was an abortive attempt to reconquer the land in 1682, but for the better part of fifteen years the Pueblos had little molestation from soldiers or friars. New Mexico was conquered again by 1696, and Indian resistance took new forms. . . . The cultural antagonism between Spaniard and Pueblo had fundamentally religious roots, and an adequate understanding of the1680 hostilities must give them priority. In the last analysis the Indian war was an attempt to preserve the kind of life which they thought the gods had ordained and which aliens were obviously destroying.—Henry Warner Bowden, "Spanish Missions, Cultural Conflict, and the Pueblo Revolt of 1680," 1975

B: [T]hese testimonies freeze for the historical record a dynamic that slowly eroded the cultural barrier separating Pueblo and European worlds. This process of acculturation would prove crucial to undercutting Spanish political authority in the region over the course of the seventeenth century. By 1680, New Mexico had become a backwash relative to the mainstream of Spanish-America colonial society; as Pueblos . . . wrought deep ethnic and cultural changes on the small European community over four generations. All vestiges of . . . dialectic of domination through physical distance and cultural segregation had vanished. Now a person of familiarity and even intimacy with the Pueblos, the Hispanic's position of authority stood in jeopardy.—Andrew L. Knaut, *The Pueblo Revolt of 1680*, 1995

Explain the difference between Interpretation A and Interpretation B:

_____

_____

_____

_____

_____

_____

Specific Historical Evidence to Support A (not mentioned in passage):

_____

_____

_____

Specific Historical Evidence to Support B (not mentioned in passage):

_____

_____

_____

_____

Interpretation: 17th-Century Puritanism

A: The colonists in New England . . . were severely handicapped in their struggle to keep up civilized standards. For the most part they were leading a tough pioneer life; their audience was small; their contacts with the centers of learning and culture in Europe were tenuous; their chances of publication were slight. But the puritans of New England did have it their own way as to the shape, the form, and the content of their intellectual life. Their tastes, desires, and prejudices dictated what would be read, studied, written, and published. Everyone knows that those tastes were in a sense narrow—for instance, they proscribed the drama. What is not sufficiently known or appreciated is this: puritanism not only did not prevent, but stimulated an interest in the classics, belles-lettres, poetry, and scientific research. Neither pioneer hardships nor other restrictions were ever so great as to prevent the burgeoning of a genuine intellectual life in that series of little beachheads on the edge of the wilderness, which was seventeenth-century New England.—Samuel Eliot Morison, *The Intellectual Life of Colonial New England*, 1956

B: [Puritan leaders] were thus attempting to found and maintain an aristocracy or oligarchy to guard a church polity which was unconsciously but implicitly democratic, their position was rendered precarious at the very outset, and increasingly so as time went on, but the necessary presence in the colony of that large unfranchised class which was not in sympathy with them. As we have seen, even under strong social and political temptation, three quarters of the population, though probably largely Puritan in sentiment and belief, persistently refused to ally themselves with the New England type of Puritan church. Their presence in the colony was undoubtedly due to economic motives, more especially perhaps, the desire to own their lands in fee. It must also have been due to economic considerations on the part of the Puritan rulers. The planting of a Bible-Commonwealth might have been possible without these non-church members, but the creation of a prosperous and populous state was not . . . it is probably that many were without strong religious motives; that few realized the plans of the leaders; and it is practically certain that the great bulk of them had never seen the charter.—James Truslow Adams, *The Founding of New England*, 1921

Explain the differences between Interpretation **A** and Interpretation **B**:

_____
_____
_____
_____
_____
_____

Specific Historical Evidence to Support **A** (not mentioned in passage):

_____
_____
_____
_____

Specific Historical Evidence to Support **B** (not mentioned in passage):

_____
_____
_____
_____

Interpretation: Jonathan Edwards and the Enlightenment

A: The truth is, Edwards was infinitely more than a theologian. He was one of America's five or six major artists, who happened to work with ideas instead of with poems or novels. He was much more a psychologist and a poet than a logician, and though he devoted his genius to topics derived from the body of divinity—the will, virtue, sin—he treated them . . . as problems not of dogma but of life. Furthermore, the conditions under which he labored, in pioneer America, make his achievement the more remarkable, and his failures the more poignant, not as an episode in the history of creeds and systems, but as a prefiguration of the artist in America. He is the child of genius in this civilization; though he met the forces of our society in their infancy, when they had not yet enlarged into the complexity we now endure . . . He maneuvered a revolt by substituting for seventeenth-century legalisms the brute language of eighteenth-century physics. He cast off habits of mind formed in feudalism, and entered abruptly into modernity, where facts rather than prescriptive rights and characters were henceforth to be the arbiters of human affairs.—Perry Miller, *Jonathan Edwards*, 1949

B: In the midst of the greatest revolution in the European mind since Christianity had overwhelmed paganism, Edwards serenely reaffirmed the faith of his fathers. He had some notion that such a revolution was going on . . . But he had no idea how extensive that revolution was, and how far his own historical thinking deviated from the historical thinking about to seize control of educated opinion in Europe. In fact, the nineteen years between Edwards' sermons and Edwards' death were decisive years in the rebellion of the Enlightenment against Christianity. . . . He was anything but an obscurantist [i.e., backward looking], and, in his feverish intellectual excitement over the ideas of Newton and Locke, he sought to express the old religion in new ways. But the results were, as they had to be, pathetic: Jonathan Edwards philosophized in a cage that his fathers had built and that he unwittingly reinforced.—Peter Gay, *A Loss of Mastery: Puritan Historians in Colonial America*, 1966

Explain the differences between Interpretation **A** and Interpretation **B**:

_____

_____

_____

_____

_____

_____

Specific Historical Evidence to Support **A** (not mentioned in passage):

_____

_____

_____

_____

Specific Historical Evidence to Support **B** (not mentioned in passage):

_____

_____

_____

_____

Interpretation: American Character

A: America is the born antagonist of Europe. I speak of the America of the United States, and of Europe such as she exists, such as she has been formed by the moulding of centuries; and not such as visionaries would like to fashion her, either after your image or after a model of their own invention. . . . you are all free, each of you is the equal of the other. Your country, then, is the classic soil of liberty and equality, and it has become so from the fact of being peopled by the men whom Europe had expelled from its bosom. That is why you, in conformity with your recent origin, and we, by a totally different genesis which is lost in the night of time, are antagonistic. . . . North America offers an unlimited field of liberty to the individual. It does not only give him the opportunity: it forces him to employ all the faculties with which God has endowed him. The area is open—as soon as he enters it he must fight, and fight to the death. In Europe it is just the contrary. Everyone finds himself hemmed in by the narrow sphere in which he is born.—Baron Graf von Hubner, *A Ramble Round the World, 1871*, 1874

B: One feature of thought and sentiment in the United States needs special examination because it has been by most observers either ignored or confounded with a phenomenon which is at bottom quite different. This is a fatalistic attitude of mind, which, since it disposes men to acquiesce in the rule of numbers, has been, when perceived, attributed to or identified with what is commonly called the Tyranny of the Majority. The tendency to fatalism is never far from mankind. . . . It has at all times formed the background to religions. No race is naturally less disposed to a fatalistic view of things than is the Anglo-American, with its restless self-reliant energy. . . . Public order becomes more easily maintained, because individuals and small groups have learned to submit even when they feel themselves aggrieved. The man who murmurs against the world, who continues to preach a hopeless cause incurs contempt, and is apt to be treated as a sort of lunatic.—James Bryce, *The American Commonwealth*, 1893

Explain the differences between Interpretation **A** and Interpretation **B**:

_____

_____

_____

_____

_____

_____

Specific Historical Evidence to Support **A** (not mentioned in passage):

_____

_____

_____

_____

Specific Historical Evidence to Support **B** (not mentioned in passage):

_____

_____

_____

_____

Interpretation: American Slavery

A: Slavery is among the oldest social systems on record. It existed in ancient China, Persia, Greece, and Rome, and biblical references to it abound. . . . Slavery survived in the northern and southern Mediterranean well into the Middle Ages. In the system's "patriarchal" form, the slave commonly worked to satisfy the limited needs of a relatively small group of people—a family or group of families . . . The arrangement thus grew out of and expressed a very primitive division of labor. . . . It began to flourish in the modern era only with the expansion of world trade. . . . Suddenly [in 1793], cotton could be grown profitably across a vast section of southern North America. By the turn of the nineteenth century, Southerners had begun the westward migration that in the next six decades would change the face of the South.—Bruce Levine, *Half Slave and Half Free: The Roots of the Civil War*, 2005

B: The history of the United States is typically told backwards, as a means of explaining to members of the current generation how their country grew to be the way it is. In such an account, slavery is a single chapter, a background event limited to one region of the country and overwhelmed by the more recent events of pioneers moving west, railroads spanning the continent, and great cities growing up around stockyards and steel mills. A history told frontwards, however, pushes slavery into the foreground, inserting it into nearly every chapter. The truth is that slavery was a national phenomenon. The North shared in the wealth it created, and in the oppression it required. . . . The North was in the perfect position, however, to deal with resistance and violence. By and large, the region's relationship with slavery, though extraordinarily profitable, was a distant one. That distance allowed the North to minimize and even deny its links with the institution that fueled its prosperity. . . . Connecticut's Harriet Beecher Stowe, author of the iconic abolitionist novel *Uncle Tom's Cabin*, said this was slavery the way Northerners liked it: all of the benefits and none of the screams.—Farrow, Lang, and Frank, *Complicity: How the North Promoted, Prolonged, and Profited from Slavery*, 2005

Explain the differences between Interpretation **A** and Interpretation **B**:

_____

_____

_____

_____

_____

_____

Specific Historical Evidence to Support **A** (not mentioned in passage):

_____

_____

_____

_____

Specific Historical Evidence to Support **B** (not mentioned in passage):

_____

_____

_____

_____

Interpretation: America's Founding

A: The American thinks highly of two essential conditions of the stable community: unity and loyalty. . . . The American political mind has never thought much along consciously radical lines. . . . The true reactionary . . . wants literally to recreate the past . . . The American Revolution was as respectful of the past as an authentic, large-scale rebellion can ever be. . . . They had little desire to make the world over. The world—at least their corner of it—had already been made over to their general satisfaction. . . . For more than three centuries all manner of Americans have fought with much success to maintain the established political and social order. . . . The ideas of the colonial Right carried over strongly into the early years of the Republic . . . Government by the favored few, the primacy of the community, reverence for the established order, aversion to change—these were the marks of the notable political philosophy, a kind of incipient American conservatism. . . . The enduring monument to their success is the American Constitution.—Clinton Rossiter, *Conservatism in America*, 1962

B: Most Americans . . . scarcely grasped the immensity of the fundamental forces at work in the Western world. They were, of course, conscious of changes and disruptions in the customs of their lives. Yet, habituated as they were to . . . stability and continuity, most were not disposed to perceive, much less understand, the structural shifts taking place in their society. . . . The imperial crisis with Great Britain and the American Revolution itself were simply clarifying incidents in this larger story of America's democratic revolution. . . . The growth and movement of people strained and broke apart households, churches, and neighborhoods. Young men particularly became more autonomous and more independent of paternal and patronage relationships. . . . Everywhere older hierarchies were broken apart and traditional paternalistic ties were severed. . . . Common people now had the financial ability to purchase "luxury" goods that previously had been the preserve of the gentry . . . distinctions of rank were even more blurred than they were in England. . . . These were the complaints of social conservatives alarmed by this conspicuous consumption and the social disorder it engendered.—Gordon S. Wood, *The Radicalism of the American Revolution*, 1991

Explain the differences between Interpretation **A** and Interpretation **B**:

_____

_____

_____

_____

_____

_____

Specific Historical Evidence to Support **A** (not mentioned in passage):

_____

_____

_____

Specific Historical Evidence to Support **B** (not mentioned in passage):

_____

_____

_____

Interpretation: Meaning of the Constitution

A: The generation that brought forth the Revolution and made the Constitution was politically the most inventive, constructive and creative in modern history. . . . Thus the Americans took the principle that men make government and institutionalized it into the constitutional convention—a mechanism which perfectly satisfied every logical requirement of that philosophical mandate. Thus they took the principle that government is limited by the laws of Nature and Nature's God, and institutionalized it into written constitutions, . . . They accepted the theory of equality—a theory that had never been accorded more than philosophical lip-service—and institutionalized it into a series of social and economic and cultural practices designed to create—almost to guarantee—a classless society.—Henry Steele Commager, *Commentary on the Constitution*, 1961

B: The Constitution of the United States was not "ordained and established" by "the people." Only a small fraction of "the people" participated in any way in the adoption of the Constitution. The Constitution was prepared in Philadelphia by a small, educated, talented, wealthy elite, representative of powerful economic interests—bondholders, investors, merchants, real estate owners, and planters. The document itself, and the new government it established, included many provisions for the protection of the elite's political and economic interests from threats by the masses. Ratification was achieved because the elite had skills and political influence disproportionate to its members. The masses of people did not participate in the adoption of the Constitution, and there is some reason to believe that these masses would have opposed the Constitution had they the information, know-how, and resources to do so. The Constitution was not a product of a popular mass movement, but instead the work of a talented, educated, wealthy, and politically skilled elite.—Thomas R. Dye and Harmon Zeigler, *The Irony of Democracy*, 1971

Explain the differences between Interpretation **A** and Interpretation **B**:

_____

_____

_____

_____

_____

_____

Specific Historical Evidence to Support **A** (not mentioned in passage):

_____

_____

_____

_____

Specific Historical Evidence to Support **B** (not mentioned in passage):

_____

_____

_____

_____

Interpretation: Meaning of the Constitution II

A: A survey of the economic interests of the members of the Convention presents certain conclusions: A majority of the members were lawyers by profession. Most of the members came from towns, on or near the coast, that is, from the regions in which personalty was largely concentrated. Not one member represented in his immediate personal economic interests the small farming or mechanic classes. The overwhelming majority of members, at least, five-sixths, were immediately, directly, and personally interested in the outcome of their labors at Philadelphia, and were to a greater or less extent economic beneficiaries from the adoption of the Constitution. . . . It cannot be said, therefore, that the members of the Convention were "disinterested." On the contrary, we are forced to accept the profoundly significant conclusion that they knew through their personal experiences in economic affairs the precise results which the new government that they were setting up was designed to attain.—Charles A. Beard, *An Economic Interpretation of the Constitution of the United States*, 1935

B: [The] men who urged and framed and advocated the Constitution were striving for an idea, an ideal—belief in a National Union, and a determination to maintain it, and the men who opposed the Constitution were also fighting for the preservation of an idea—self-rule as opposed to control by a central government which they feared would destroy their local governments. Historians who leave these factors out of account and who contend that these men were moved chiefly by economic conditions utterly fail to interpret their character and their acts. . . . That they realized the disastrous economic conditions, that they feared the effect of prevailing unwise and unjust State legislation, and that they expected that a more adequate form of Government would bring an increase of economic prosperity for all classes in the community, cannot be doubted. But it is equally indubitable that their leading motive in desiring a new Constitution was their conviction that, without it, a dissolution of the Union and disappearance of republican government were inevitable.—Charles Warren, *The Making of the Constitution*, 1947

Explain the differences between Interpretation **A** and Interpretation **B**:

_____

_____

_____

_____

_____

_____

Specific Historical Evidence to Support **A** (not mentioned in passage):

_____

_____

_____

_____

Specific Historical Evidence to Support **B** (not mentioned in passage):

_____

_____

_____

_____

Interpretation: Development of the First Political Parties

A: Jefferson set out to enlist a large following in his struggle against the capitalistic measures of Hamilton. He made his strongest appeal directly to the agriculturalists of the country. And when his party was fully organized he took pride in saying that "the whole landed interest is republican," that is, lined up on his side of the contest. . . . Appealing to the farmers and the masses in general against the larger capitalistic interests, Jefferson's party inevitably took a popular, that is, a democratic turn. This was in keeping with his theories, for he thought that kings, clergy, nobles, and other ruling classes of Europe had filled their countries with poverty and misery and kept the world in turmoil with useless wars. The common people, he reasoned, if given liberty and let alone, would be happier under their own government than under any ruling class. . . . Rustic simplicity [and] *laissez faire* . . . such were the chief political articles among the professions of Jeffersonian Republicans.—Charles A. Beard, *The Economic Basis of Politics and Related Writings*, 1922

B: The Federalist Party was modern in that it was a relatively open, regularized political structure built around the free association of men from various walks of life, who evolved rationalized methods as efficient means to political goals and, in the era of emerging popular participation in politics, turned to propaganda and campaign tactics aimed at the mass of voters. It was modern also in the way in which its leaders and cadre workers devised orderly procedures to meet the claims of the plurality of interest groups thrown up by a developing economy, undertook to perform key political functions in a coordinated, regularized, consistent manner and offered a generalized ideology and program. . . . In one aspect after another, the Federalists in their time represented a distinctively new kind of political engine and realized in practice the major themes of political modernization.—William Nisbet Chambers, *Political Parties in a New Nation: The American Experience, 1776–1809*, 1963

Explain the differences between Interpretation **A** and Interpretation **B**:

_____

_____

_____

_____

_____

_____

Specific Historical Evidence to Support **A** (not mentioned in passage):

_____

_____

_____

_____

Specific Historical Evidence to Support **B** (not mentioned in passage):

_____

_____

_____

_____

Interpretation: Causes of the War of 1812

A: The rise of Tecumseh, backed, as was universally believed, by the British, produced an urgent demand in the Northwest that the British be expelled from Canada. This demand was a factor of primary importance in bringing on the war. . . . Even within the Republican Party, there was already a distinct sectional rift between North and South, and neither section was anxious to see the other increase its territory and population. But if both could gain at the same time, and in something like equal proportion, such objections would be obviated on both sides. . . . Thus the war began with a double-barreled scheme of territorial aggrandizement . . . . Finally, in the expansionist program with which the war opened, we have the first general appearance of the idea which later received the name of "Manifest Destiny."—Julius W. Pratt, *Expansionists of 1812*, 1925

B: The modern tendency to seek materialistic motives and economic factors in all human relations has greatly obscured one of the basic causes of the War of 1812. . . . a cursory glance at the statistics of American commerce in the first decade of the nineteenth century will show that the War of 1812 was the most uneconomic war the United States has ever fought. A casual search through the letters and speeches of contemporaries reveals that those who fought the war were primarily concerned with the honor and integrity of the nation. . . . The war hawks, it is true, provided with their skill and energy the necessary impetus to war, but they could not have done so had not a majority of the Republican Party, particularly in the South, become gradually converted to the idea that war was the only alternative to national humiliation and disgrace.—Norman K. Risjord, "1812: Conservatives, War Hawks, and the Nation's Honor," 1961

Explain the differences between Interpretation **A** and Interpretation **B**:

_____

_____

_____

_____

_____

_____

Specific Historical Evidence to Support **A** (not mentioned in passage):

_____

_____

_____

_____

Specific Historical Evidence to Support **B** (not mentioned in passage):

_____

_____

_____

_____

Interpretation: Monroe Doctrine

A: The message of President Monroe was welcomed with great rejoicing throughout Latin America. Not knowing the inside story of the diplomatic negotiations which preceded it, not knowing the weakness of the European menace at that time, not knowing the real purpose of the Washington government in advancing it, the people of Latin America attributed to the Monroe Doctrine a degree of altruism and effectiveness far above reality. Only through the glass of this popular delusion, the efforts of the most important Latin American governments of the epoch to participate in the privileges and obligations of the Doctrine may be understood. They evidently overestimated the generosity of their Northern neighbor and misunderstood its aims. . . . Their mistaken optimism, on the other hand, and the disappointment which it caused them, served to clarify the real nature of the Monroe declarations and to establish even then, at the very beginning, the light in which the United States looked upon those declarations.—Gaston Nerval, *Autopsy of the Monroe Doctrine*, 1934

B: A century after the announcement of the Doctrine, one of our most eminent Secretaries of State, Charles Evans Hughes—who, it should be noted, through continuing non-recognition of Soviet Russia pointed to the essentially malign nature of Communism—stated the modern meaning of the Monroe Doctrine. "It still remains, to be applied if necessary, as a principle of national security. . . . [it is] an integral part of national thought and purpose expressing a profound conviction which even the upheaval caused by the world war, and the participation of the United States in that struggle on European soil, did not upset." At this moment it should be understood that the Doctrine applies not just to the acquisition of territory, but to the extension of a "system." . . . Now there is not merely a threat but an actual, demonstrable fact that the Communist system is established in Cuba and in strong Communist movements in other Latin American nations. . . . The Monroe Doctrine is an "entailed" inheritance. It cannot be sold for the promise of good will nor given away, nor dissipated by reinterpretation. Those who speak for the nation now are not creators, they are trustees.—Raymond Moley, "Perspective," 1962

Explain the differences between Interpretation **A** and Interpretation **B**:

_____

_____

_____

_____

_____

_____

Specific Historical Evidence to Support **A** (not mentioned in passage):

_____

_____

_____

_____

Specific Historical Evidence to Support **B** (not mentioned in passage):

_____

_____

_____

_____

Interpretation: Jacksonian Democracy

A: The secret of his [i.e., Andrew Jackson's] power was his adjustment to the period in which he lived. Other men excelled him in experience, wisdom, and balanced judgment; but the American democrats of the day admired neither of these qualities. They honored courage, strength, and directness. They could tolerate ignorance but not hesitancy. Jackson was the best embodiment of their desires from the beginning of the national government to his own day. Jackson accepted democracy with relentless logic. Some others believed that wise leaders could best determine the policies of government, but he more than anyone else of his day threw the task of judging upon the common man. . . . Jackson's lack of education, his crude judgments in many affairs, his occasional outbreaks of passion, his habitual hatred of those enemies with whom he had not made friends for party purposes, and his crude ideas of some political policies—all lose some of their infelicity in the face of his brave, frank, masterly leadership of the democratic movement which then established itself in our life. . . . Few American Presidents have better lived up to the demands of the movement which brought them into power.—John Spencer Bassett, *The Life of Andrew Jackson*, 1911

B: On December 10 the President issued a Proclamation against the Nullifiers. . . . In terse and commanding prose the Proclamation declared that the National Government was sovereign and indivisible, that no state could refuse to obey the law, that no state could leave the Union. . . . Yet able and powerful as it was, it went too far for its purpose and its time. Its reasoning, though cogent and compelling, destroyed not nullification alone, but the whole theory of State Rights from which the doctrine of interposition had been derived. When it proclaimed the government to be no federation but a consolidated whole with sovereign power vested in the majority, it went far beyond the purposes of the founding fathers, and ran directly counter to widely accepted beliefs of the time. The net effect, therefore, was not to isolate the leaders in South Carolina but to arouse all those who feared concentrated power, by whomsoever exercised. New party lines were drawn, and the Nullifiers found support where none had been expected.—Charles M. Wiltse, *John C. Calhoun, Nullifier, 1829–1839*, 1949

Explain the differences between Interpretation **A** and Interpretation **B**:

_____

_____

_____

_____

_____

_____

Specific Historical Evidence to Support **A** (not mentioned in passage):

_____

_____

_____

Specific Historical Evidence to Support **B** (not mentioned in passage):

_____

_____

_____

_____

Interpretation: Cherokee Removal

A: In the whole history of our Government's dealings with the Indian tribes, there is no record so black as the record of its perfidy to this nation. . . . There is no instance in all history of a race of people passing in so short a space of time from the barbarous stage to the agricultural and civilized. And it was such a community as this that the State of Georgia, by one high-handed outrage, made outlaws! . . . [The Supreme Court] held that the Cherokee tribe did constitute a foreign nation, and that the State of Georgia ought to be enjoined from execution of its unjust laws. . . . But all this did not help the Cherokees; . . . Fierce factions began to be formed in the nation, one for and one against the surrender of their lands. Many were ready still to remain and suffer till death rather than give them up; but wiser counsels prevailed, and in the last days of the year 1835 a treaty was concluded with the United States . . . [which] relinquished all the lands clamed or possessed by them east of the Mississippi River.—Helen Hunt Jackson, *A Century of Dishonor*, 1881

B: The Cherokees, living in the mountainous part of the state to the northward, had not got in the way of the Georgians as quickly as had the Creeks; but Georgia was no less conscious of their presence and no less determined that they also must go. . . . the Cherokees began to take on a national consciousness and to consider themselves forever implanted in the lower ramparts of their beloved Southern highlands, in a region which had been claimed by Georgians from the day George II had granted it in 1732 . . . This threat of being deprived of a great part of her domain by an alien and semi-barbarous people appeared intolerable and unthinkable to Georgia; she would resist it to the uttermost limits. . . . Thought Georgia was not the only state to have Indians, she had greater difficulty than any other in getting rid of them or settling the question of their status . . . With the Indians finally out of the way, Georgia was for the first time in her existence master of her own territorial destiny. Now she was unshackled; with exuberance and enthusiasm she could now go forward.—E. Merton Coulter, *Georgia, a Short History*, 1947

Explain the differences between Interpretation **A** and Interpretation **B**:

_____

_____

_____

_____

_____

_____

Specific Historical Evidence to Support **A** (not mentioned in passage):

_____

_____

_____

_____

Specific Historical Evidence to Support **B** (not mentioned in passage):

_____

_____

_____

_____

Interpretation: Abolitionism in the North

A: To be an abolitionist was to declare allegiance to the principles of brotherhood and equality of opportunity, to suffer for those ideals, and to band together with like-minded individuals. It was to find a moral community in a society that appeared increasingly immoral. Antislavery also attracted support because it spoke to a complex set of hopes and fears about the future. These were social in origin and they were expressed forcefully in a kind of moral drama present in much abolitionist propaganda. . . . Most of these assumptions were familiar to Americans and permeated other reforms of the day. . . . Race prejudice prevented the majority of Northern whites from acknowledging how thoroughly antislavery expressed many of their own cherished economic and religious beliefs. . . . The war disturbed many Northerners who cared nothing for black people and who were not especially hostile to the South. So long as slavery stayed where it was, they could tolerate it and comfort themselves by believing it would die a natural death.—Ronald G. Walters, *American Reformers, 1815–1860*, 1978

B: To have adopted the path of direct abolition, first of all, might have meant risking individual respectability. The unsavory reputation of those already associated with abolitionism was not likely to encourage converts to it. . . . Immediatism challenged the Northern hierarchy of values. To many, a direct assault on slavery meant a direct assault on private property and the Union . . . If property could not be protected in a nation, neither could life nor liberty. . . . By 1840 . . . most abolitionists had become immediatists, and that position, "practical" or not, did have a compelling moral urgency. Men learned how to be free, the immediatists argued, only by being free; slavery, no matter how attenuated, was by its very nature incapable of preparing men for those independent decisions necessary to adult responsibility. . . . Those Northerners who were not indifferent to slavery—a large number after 1845—were nonetheless prone to view the abolitionist protest as "excessive," for it threatened the cherished values of private property and Union.—Martin Duberman, "The Northern Response to Slavery," 1965

Explain the differences between Interpretation **A** and Interpretation **B**:

_____

_____

_____

_____

_____

_____

Specific Historical Evidence to Support **A** (not mentioned in passage):

_____

_____

_____

Specific Historical Evidence to Support **B** (not mentioned in passage):

_____

_____

_____

Interpretation: Mexican War

A: The pacific expansionist who rejoiced in the bloodless annexation of Texas was shortly mocked by the resultant war with the aggrieved recent owner of that disputed country. The War with Mexico was in turn the cause of a new territorial ambition which, though it resulted merely in the acquisition of New Mexico and Upper California, was directed for a time toward the annexation of all Mexico and fell short of it only through a slight turn of events. This ambition marked a momentous change both in the policy and in the ideal of American expansionism. . . . the enlargement of territorial aim was probably due less to philanthropy than to a consideration of national self-interest. . . . Yet the expansionism of the Mexican War anticipated the ideology of the white man's burden by accepting the obligation to the darker peoples. Expansionists contemplated not merely the regeneration of the Mexicans but a whole series of civilizing enterprises among the lesser breeds.—Albert K. Weinberg, *Manifest Destiny*, 1935

B: An old age was dying, a new age being born; and such stormy transitions always bear harshly upon party structures. Facing the new issues which the war created, both Whigs and Democrats showed the strain. Being in power, the Democratic Party suffered the more. A few years earlier it had seemed homogeneous and closely knit. Actually, it was composed of disparate interests bound together by very loose ties and ready to quarrel the moment a sufficient motive appeared; and now the war revealed its essential lack of unity. A powerful body of Northern Democrats, their greatest strength lying in New England and upper New York, stood opposed to any expansion of slavery. A still more powerful body of Southern Democrats, counting many Northern supporters, held that slavery had right to spread through any areas where climate and other conditions favored it. Alongside these two bodies stood a vigorous array of Democrats, their principal strength in the northwest, who were not unwilling to allow slavery to grow if by some compromise free soil grew with equal or greater celerity.—Allen Nevins, *Ordeal of the Union*, 1950

Explain the differences between Interpretation **A** and Interpretation **B**:

_____

_____

_____

_____

_____

_____

Specific Historical Evidence to Support **A** (not mentioned in passage):

_____

_____

_____

_____

Specific Historical Evidence to Support **B** (not mentioned in passage):

_____

_____

_____

_____

Interpretation: Causes of the Civil War

A: Had the economic systems of the North and South remained static or changed slowly without effecting immense dislocations in the social structure, the balance of power might have been maintained indefinitely by repeating the compensatory tactics of 1787, 1820, 1833, and 1850; . . . But nothing was stable in the economy of the United States or in the moral sentiments associated with its diversities. Within each section of the country, the necessities of the productive system were generating portentous results. . . . the Northeast was daily enlarging, agriculture in the Northwest was being steadily supplemented by manufacturing, and the area of virgin soil open to exploitation by planters was diminishing with rhythmic regularity. . . . Given an irrepressible conflict which could be symbolized in such unmistakable patterns by competent interpreters of opposing factions, a transfer of the issues from the forum to the field, from the conciliation of diplomacy to the decision of arms was bound to come.—Charles A. Beard, *The Rise of American Civilization*, 1933

B: Thus war came when the American people for the first time refused to abide by a national election. The parties which had been promoting the cohesive attitudes had broken down . . . The social, economic, and cultural differences had been so used by the political operators as to produce secession and civil war. War broke out because no means had been devised to curb the extravagant use of the divisive forces. Statesmanship seemed poverty-stricken. The work of the nationalists who sought to find a formula with which to overcome the divisive attitudes was vain. Too few even saw the need for the formula; they ran heedlessly down the path to disruption. The war was the product of the chaotic lack of system in ascertaining and directing the public will, a chaos exploited with little regard for the welfare of the general public by irresponsible and blind operators.—Roy F. Nichols, *The Disruption of American Democracy*, 1948

Explain the differences between Interpretation **A** and Interpretation **B**:

_____

_____

_____

_____

_____

_____

Specific Historical Evidence to Support **A** (not mentioned in passage):

_____

_____

_____

_____

Specific Historical Evidence to Support **B** (not mentioned in passage):

_____

_____

_____

_____

Interpretation: Causes of the Civil War II

A: In the summer of 1850 Americans looked out upon their country with eyes that glowed with pride and confidence. . . . [Both the North and the South] had reached a high degree of self-consciousness and it had seemed that their interests might be mutually antagonistic, especially in determining the future of the new land gained from Mexico and thus of national control. . . . For the most part the South, hampered by its caste system, its undigested mass of poor whites and enslaved blacks, its growing antagonism to the free states, remained unaffected by the new currents of civilization. It did not share in the movement for popular education . . . it had little of a creative nature to contribute to science, scholarship, letters and the arts. More and more it lived to itself, closed in by tradition and by loyalty to a social institution which it alone in all the civilized world maintained and defended. The widening breach between the sections thus reached beyond political acerbities into the very substance of life itself.—Arthur C. Cole, *The Irrepressible Conflict, 1850–1865*, 1934

B: If the negro had never been brought to America and enslaved, South Carolina would not have seceded. Nothing in all history is plainer than that the ferment of which I have been speaking was due solely to the existence of slavery. That the North had been encroaching upon the South, that it had offered an indignity in the election of Lincoln, was for South Carolinians a feeling perfectly natural, and it was absolutely sincere. The President-elect believed that slavery should ultimately be done away with, while they were convinced that it was either a blessing, or else the only fit and possible condition of the negro in contact with the white. That their cause was the cause of life, liberty, and property seemed, from their point of view, beyond question.—James Ford Rhodes, *History of the United States from the Compromise of 1850*, 1895

Explain the differences between Interpretation **A** and Interpretation **B**:

_____

_____

_____

_____

_____

_____

Specific Historical Evidence to Support **A** (not mentioned in passage):

_____

_____

_____

Specific Historical Evidence to Support **B** (not mentioned in passage):

_____

_____

_____

Interpretation: Fate of the Confederacy

A: So the Confederacy succumbed to internal rather than external causes. An insufficient nationalism had to survive the strains imposed by the lengthy hostilities. . . . Slavery, in a sense the keystone of secession, became a liability as the Union's fight against slavery and the South's own religious beliefs induced more guilt among more southerners. After three years of essentially successful defense against powerful invading forces, these prolonged strains proved more than Confederate nationalism could bear and, frequently encouraged by a sense that defeat must be the Lord's work, Confederates, by thousands of individual decisions, abandoned the struggle for and allegiance to the Confederate States of America. And yet . . . Southerners eventually resolved the dissonance between the world as it was and the world as they had wanted it to be by securing enough of their war aims—state rights, white supremacy, and honor—to permit them to claim their share of the victory. Richard E. Beringer et al., *Why the South Lost the Civil War*, 1986

B: Most attempts to explain southern defeat or northern victory lack the dimension of contingency—the recognition that at numerous critical points during the war things might have gone altogether differently. . . . Northern victory and southern defeat in the war cannot be understood apart from the contingency that hung over every campaign, every battle, every election, every decision during the war. James M. McPherson, *The Illustrated Battle Cry of Freedom*, 2003

Explain the difference between Interpretation A and Interpretation B:

_____

_____

_____

_____

_____

_____

Specific Historical Evidence to Support A (not mentioned in passage):

_____

_____

_____

_____

Specific Historical Evidence to Support B (not mentioned in passage):

_____

_____

_____

_____

Interpretation: Assessment of Lincoln's Presidency

A: After careful consideration of our own case, I do not hesitate to condemn the arbitrary arrests and the arbitrary interference with the freedom of the press in States which were not the theatre of the war and where the courts were open [as well as other instances of blatant disregard for the Constitution]. . . . I am convinced that all of this extrajudicial procedure was inexpedient, unnecessary, and wrong; that the offenders should have been prosecuted according to law, or, if their offences were not indictable, permitted to go free. . . . While I have not lighted upon an instance in which the President himself directed an arrest, he permitted them all; he stands responsible for the casting into prison of citizens of the United States on order as arbitrary as the *lettres-de-cachet* of Louis XIV.—James Ford Rhodes, *History of the United States from the Compromise of 1850*, 1893–1906

B: Lincoln's primary task as a politician was to create a national Republican Party and to mold it into a serviceable tool for the national welfare. The party which nominated him and put him into the White House was an unorganized conglomeration of opposition groups. . . . The mandate of the Republican Party was far from clear, and even had Lincoln attempted to conform to its vague provisions, it would have furnished no practical guide to the political situation which confronted him. There was, in fact, no national Republican Party. . . . Lincoln made no effort to assume leadership in legislation. He had, indeed, no legislative program to promote, and faced none of the problems of the legislative leader who needed to bargain and cajole, to coerce and to compromise to get support for a bill. On the other hand, he had a war to conduct and needed the support of an integrated national party to bring it to a successful conclusion. . . . Fully aware of the contending factions, Lincoln delayed calling Congress into session until four months after his inauguration. . . . this act gave the party a program and brought conciliators and compromisers among the politicians into line. . . . Lincoln had, indeed, built a national party. He had used the patronage, the prestige of his position, the army, and skillful popular appeals to subordinate the state parties and mold them into national unity.—William B. Hesseltine, "Abraham Lincoln and the Politicians," 1960

Explain the differences between Interpretation **A** and Interpretation **B**:

_____

_____

_____

_____

_____

Specific Historical Evidence to Support **A** (not mentioned in passage):

_____

_____

_____

Specific Historical Evidence to Support **B** (not mentioned in passage):

_____

_____

_____

Interpretation: Reconstruction

A: The process of creating a new electorate and through it a new government in each of the ten states was carried on by the . . . radical spirit of the reconstruction acts. The registration of voters was so directed as to insure beyond all peradventure the fullest enrollment of the blacks and the completest exclusion of disfranchised whites. . . . The most conspicuous feature of maladministration was that of the finances. . . . all these works absorbed large sums and were unopposed by the conservatives, save where extravagance and corruption were manifest or suspected. . . . In most of the reconstructed states the very first term of the radical administration developed a schism in the party in power. In a general way the line of this cleavage was that dividing the southern white from the northern white element. . . . As the negroes caught the spirit of politics and demanded more and more of the positions and essential power in their party, the southern whites could not bring themselves to the same amount of concessions [as northerners] . . . the negro had no pride of race and no aspiration or ideals save to be like the whites. With civil rights and political power, not won, but almost forced upon him, he came gradually to understand and crave those more elusive privileges that constitute social equality. . . . But every form and suggestion of social equality was resented and resisted by the whites with the energy of despair. The dread of it justified in their eyes modes of lawlessness which were wholly subversive of civilization.— William A. Dunning, *Reconstruction, Political and Economic, 1865–1877*, 1907

B: Thus radical rule, in spite of its shortcomings, was by no means synonymous with incompetence and corruption; far too many carpetbagger, scalawag, and Negro politicians made creditable records to warrant such a generalization. Moreover, conditions were improving in the final years of reconstruction. . . . Finally, granting all their mistakes, the radical governments were by far the most democratic the South had ever known. They were the only governments in southern history to extend to Negroes complete civil and political equality, and to try to protect then in the enjoyment of the rights they were granted.—Kenneth M. Stampp, *The Era of Reconstruction*, 1965

Explain the differences between Interpretation **A** and Interpretation **B**:

_____

_____

_____

_____

_____

_____

Specific Historical Evidence to Support **A** (not mentioned in passage):

_____

_____

_____

Specific Historical Evidence to Support **B** (not mentioned in passage):

_____

_____

_____

_____

Interpretation: Reconstruction II

A: In the end . . . neither the abolition of slavery nor Reconstruction succeeded in resolving the debate over the meaning of freedom in American life. . . . And in the United States, as in nearly every plantation society that experienced the end of slavery, a rigid social and political dichotomy between former master and former slave, an ideology of racism, and a dependent labor force with limited economic opportunities all survived abolition. . . . Yet by the same token . . . the United States, for a moment, offered the freedmen a measure of political control over their own destinies. However brief its sway, Reconstruction allowed scope for a remarkable political and social mobilization of the black community. It opened doors of opportunity that could never be completely closed. Reconstruction transformed the lives of Southern blacks in ways unmeasurable . . . It raised their expectations and aspirations, redefined their status in relation to the larger society, and allowed space for the creation of institutions that enabled them to survive the repression that followed. And it established constitutional principles of civil and political equality that, while flagrantly violated after Reconstruction, planted the seeds of future struggle. Eric Foner, "The New View of Reconstruction." 1983

B: Had Lincoln in the course of a second term succeeded in obtaining a far broader consent from the white South to terms that would satisfy northern Republican opinion than did Congress in 1867-1869, ultimate victory in the battle over the ex-slave's status as free man would not necessarily have followed. There would still have been the need to build institutions that could safeguard and expand what had been won—laws that the courts would uphold, and economy offering escape from poverty and dependency, a Union-Republican part in the South recognized by its opponents as a legitimate contestant for political power. The opportunities open to Lincoln for institutionalizing gains made toward equal citizenship irrespective of color were limited. . . . The concepts and perceptions then dominant, although not unreasonable on the basis of past experience, were inadequate to meet the challenge of transforming the South. LaWanda Cox, *Lincoln and Black Freedom: A Study in Presidential Leadership*, 1981

Explain the difference between Interpretation A and Interpretation B:

_____

_____

_____

_____

_____

Specific Historical Evidence to Support A (not mentioned in passage):

_____

_____

_____

Specific Historical Evidence to Support B (not mentioned in passage):

_____

_____

_____

Interpretation: Robber Barons

A: While the productive labors of a society, the functioning of its ships and railroads, its mills and factories, give the effect of a beautiful order and discipline, of the rhythmic regularity of the days and seasons, its markets, by a strange contrast, seem to be in a continual state of anarchy. Here the same services and commodities, produced everyday with perfect routine, go through a mad dance. . . . Jay Gould seems the capitalist par excellence. During all the heroic, turbulent period we review he seems the very soul of the movement of industrial revolution. . . . Where certain of his rivals, intoxicated with power, learned to crave glory too, Jay Gould seemed to place himself above such human vanities. Nor did any social interest, or any sentimental consideration, as the size or beauty of an enterprise, deflect him for a moment from his marvelously logical line of movement. No human instinct of justice or patriotism or pity caused him to deceive himself, or to waver in any perceptible degree from the stead-fast pursuit of strategic power.—Matthew Josephson, *The Robber Barons*, 1936

B: In assessing the importance of a business leader, his contribution to the industry and to the public welfare must be considered. This is particularly true in an examination of business success in the free-enterprise economy of the period following the Civil War. . . . It is therefore particularly profitable to examine the contributions made both in terms of business advance and public service which were made by Gould in the generation following the Civil War. Gould was, and still remains, a business type. He had his virtues and he had his faults. . . . the public benefited from his activities as a man of business in the railroad industry and in the field of speculative capital. As a leader in the railroad industry he built many new roads; he broke down local territorial monopolies, destroyed traffic pools, and wrecked railroad rate structures. . . . The public did gain permanently, so far as anything permanent can be assumed to exist in economic life. . . . To Gould, as much as to any other single business leader, goes the credit for that far-reaching reduction in rates that characterized the growth of the American economy in the generation after the Civil War.—Julius Grodinsky, *Jay Gould, His Business Career, 1867–1892*, 1957

Explain the differences between Interpretation **A** and Interpretation **B**:

_____

_____

_____

_____

_____

_____

Specific Historical Evidence to Support **A** (not mentioned in passage):

_____

_____

_____

_____

Specific Historical Evidence to Support **B** (not mentioned in passage):

_____

_____

_____

_____

Interpretation: Frontier in American History

A: Up to our own day American history has been in a large degree the history of the colonization of the Great West. The existence of an area of free land, its continuous recession, and the advance of American settlement westward, explain American development. Behind institutions, behind constitutional forms and modifications, lie the vital forces that call these organs into life, and shape them to meet changing conditions. . . . American social development has been continually beginning over again on the frontier. This perennial rebirth, the fluidity of American life, this expansion westward with its new opportunities, its continuous touch with the simplicity of primitive society, furnish the forces dominating American character. The true point of view in the history of this nation is not the Atlantic coast, it is the Great West. . . . The most important effect of the frontier has been in the promotion of democracy here and in Europe. As has been pointed out, the frontier is productive of individualism.—Frederick Jackson Turner, "The Significance of the Frontier in American History," 1893

B: Conventional frontier theory never made much room for the West beyond the hundredth meridian. Any number of central characteristics of that region played either a limited role, or no role at all . . . Western aridity is only the most obvious. The continued presence and resistance to conquest of Indian people; Spanish settlement in the Southwest preceding Anglo-American settlement anywhere in North America as well as the continued give-and-take between Latin America and Anglo America; the industrial reality of much western mining; Asian immigration and the West's involvement in the Pacific Rim; ongoing disputes over the ownership and management of public lands; the existence of something other than the ideal pioneer democracy and equality in western state and local governments—most of these central items found their homes on the edges of the field, if they found any home at all.—Patricia Nelson Limerick, "What on Earth Is the New Western History?," 1990

Explain the differences between Interpretation **A** and Interpretation **B**:

_____
_____
_____
_____
_____
_____

Specific Historical Evidence to Support **A** (not mentioned in passage):

_____
_____
_____
_____

Specific Historical Evidence to Support **B** (not mentioned in passage):

_____
_____
_____
_____

Interpretation: Populists

A: For a generation after the Civil War, a time of great economic exploitation and waste, grave social corruption and ugliness, the dominant note in American political life was complacency. Although dissenting minorities were always present, they were submerged by the overwhelming realities of industrial growth and continental settlement. The agitation of the Populists, which brought back to American public life a capacity for effective political indignation, marks the beginning of the end of this epoch. In the short run the Populists did not get what they wanted, but they released the flow of protest and criticism that swept through American political affairs from the 1890's to the beginning of the first World War.—Richard Hofstadter, *The Age of Reform*, 1955

B: The remarkable strength the Populists manifested in the Lower South was gained against far more formidable obstacles than any ever encountered in the West. For there they daily faced the implacable dogmas of racism, white solidarity, white supremacy, and the bloody shirt. . . . They had to contend regularly with foreclosure of mortgages, discharge from jobs, eviction as tenants, exclusion from church, withholding of credit, boycott, social ostracism, and the endlessly reiterated charge of racial disloyalty and sectional disloyalty. . . . Having waged their revolt at such great cost, the Southern Populists were far less willing to compromise their principles than were their Western brethren. It was the Western Populists who planned and led the movement to sell out the party to the Silverites, and the Southern Populists who fought and resisted the drift to quasi-Populism. The Southerners were consistently more radical, more insistent upon their economic reforms, and more stubbornly unwilling to lose their party identity in the watered down quasi-Populism of Bryan than were the Westerners. . . . Whatever their concern the farmers might have had for their status was overwhelmed by desperate and immediate economic anxieties. While their legislative program may have often been naïve and inadequate, it was almost obsessively economic and, as political platforms go, little more irrational than the run-of-the-mill.—C. Vann Woodward, *The Burden of Southern History*, 1960

Explain the differences between Interpretation **A** and Interpretation **B**:

_____

_____

_____

_____

_____

_____

Specific Historical Evidence to Support **A** (not mentioned in passage):

_____

_____

_____

_____

Specific Historical Evidence to Support **B** (not mentioned in passage):

_____

_____

_____

_____

Interpretation: Causes of the Spanish-American War

A: The decade of the 1890's which witnessed the final crisis of the long continued friction between Spain and her Cuban colony marked also the appearance of a new type of journalism in New York City. While a number of veteran newspaper men were grimly attempting to maintain conservative standards, a new school in newspaper making with its reckless headlines, "popular" features, and sensational appeals to the masses reached many readers previously impervious to the comparatively staid sheets of the old order. . . . The outbreak of the Cuban revolution came at an opportune time for the newspaper . . . . The sensational newspapers were fully alive to the public's excited interest . . . and made frantic efforts to get—or manufacture—the news, and to present it in the most lurid fashion. . . . The Spanish-American War . . . was a popular crusade. Neither the business interests of the nation nor the Government executives desired it. The public, aroused by the press, demanded it.—Joseph E. Wisan, *The Cuban Crisis as Reflected in the New York Press*, 1934

B: The Philippine crisis is inseparable from the [Spanish American War] crisis, and the war crisis itself is inseparable from a larger constellation that might be called "the psychic crisis of the 1890's." Central in the background of the psychic crisis was the great depression that broke . . . and was still very acute when the agitation over the war in Cuba began. . . . These symptoms fall into two basic moods. The key to one of them is an intensification of protest and humanitarian reform. . . . The other is one of national self-assertion, aggression, expansion. The tone of the first was sympathy, of the second, power. . . . I suspect that the readiness of the public to over-react to the Cuban situation can be understood in part through the displacement of feelings of sympathy or social protest generated in domestic affairs; these impulses found a safe and satisfactory discharge in foreign conflict.—Richard Hofstadter, "Manifest Destiny and the Philippines," 1952

Explain the differences between Interpretation **A** and Interpretation **B**:

_____

_____

_____

_____

_____

_____

Specific Historical Evidence to Support **A** (not mentioned in passage):

_____

_____

_____

Specific Historical Evidence to Support **B** (not mentioned in passage):

_____

_____

_____

_____

Interpretation: William Jennings Bryan

A: William Jennings Bryan . . . Here was a man who maintained himself in a position of very great political power for a generation, without a political organization, without wealth except his own earnings, without holding office except for a brief period . . . Other men have been far more powerful at given moment than Bryan, but maintained his ascendancy over the minds of millions of voters for so sustained a period as the Nebraska statesman. . . . Bryan represented the West and the South as against the East and the Center of the country, and voiced their demand for drastic measures to help the agrarian, debtor communities. . . . Bryan felt the current of popular movements with great sensitiveness. . . . his strength was peculiarly recruited from the agrarian group, the labor group, and the religious group. . . . He was neither a demagogue, nor a great constructive statesman, but he was the greatest political evangelist of his day—a prophet whose voice was raised again and again against the abuses of the time in which he lived.—Charles E. Merriam, *Four American Party Leaders*, 1926

B: William Jennings Bryan's last secular act on this globe of sin was to catch flies. . . . He knew every country town in the South and West, and he could crowd the most remote of them to suffocation by simply winding his horn. . . . Bryan lived too long, and descended too deeply into the mud, to be taken seriously hereafter by fully literate men . . . His career brought him into contact with the first men of his time; he preferred the company of rustic ignoramuses . . . he fought his last fight [i.e., the Scopes Trial], thirsting savagely for blood. All sense departed from him. He bit right and left, like a dog with rabies. He descended to demagogy so dreadful that his very associates at the trial table blushed. . . . The President of the United States may be an ass, but he at least doesn't believe that the earth is square, and that witches should be put to death, and that Jonah swallowed the whale. The Golden Text is not painted weekly on the White House wall . . . We have escaped something—by a narrow margin, but still we have escaped.—H.L. Mencken, "In Memoriam: W.J.B.," 1926

Explain the differences between Interpretation **A** and Interpretation **B**:

_____

_____

_____

_____

_____

_____

Specific Historical Evidence to Support **A** (not mentioned in passage):

_____

_____

_____

_____

Specific Historical Evidence to Support **B** (not mentioned in passage):

_____

_____

_____

_____

Interpretation: Immigration and the Melting Pot

A: To live in America, then, is to live in the atmosphere of these immaterial standards and values, to possess them in one's own character, and to be possessed by them. This means to live in close, spontaneous, daily contact with genuine Americans. For the native-born American of American ancestry, as already stated, this is natural and automatic. What is it for the foreign immigrant? . . . The process of Americanization . . . for the immigrant is infinitely more difficult than for the native because the former, during the years before his arrival in the United States, has already acquired more or less completely a foreign nationality. This nationality is dissimilar in most respects, and absolutely contradictory and inconsistent in many respects, to the American nationality. . . . Let the critical and self-satisfied American of native birth reflect that in the process of Americanization this whole spiritual endowment must be abandoned.—Henry Pratt Fairchild, *The Melting-Pot Mistake*, 1926

B: There is a culture in the United States and not an ignoble one . . . It is founded upon variation of racial groups and individual character; upon spontaneous differences of social heritage, institutional habit, mental attitude and emotional tone; upon the continuous, free and fruitful cross-fertilization of these by one another. Within these Many, gathered upon the American scene from the four corners of the earth and taking root and finding nourishment, growth and integrity upon its soil, lies the American One, as poets, painters, musicians and philosophers feel and utter this One From the days when the New England school first turned its heart to Europe for spiritual sustenance and workmanlike guidance to the days when all the culture enclaves of Europe began to make a new life upon the North American continent, the culture of the United States has gathered volume and headway; has gathered variety, color and significance.—Horace M. Kallen, *Culture and Democracy in the United States*, 1951

Explain the differences between Interpretation **A** and Interpretation **B**:

_____

_____

_____

_____

_____

_____

Specific Historical Evidence to Support **A** (not mentioned in passage):

_____

_____

_____

Specific Historical Evidence to Support **B** (not mentioned in passage):

_____

_____

_____

Interpretation: The Progressives

A: Populism had been overwhelmingly rural and provincial. The ferment of the Progressive era was urban, middle-class, and nation-wide. Above all, Progressivism differed from Populism in the fact that the middle classes of the cities not only joined the trend toward protest but took over its leadership. While Bryan's old followers still kept their interest in certain reforms, they now found themselves in the company of large numbers who had hitherto violently opposed them. As the demand for reform spread from the farmers to the middle class and from the Populist Party into the major parties, it became more powerful and more highly regarded. It had been possible for their enemies to brand the Populists as wild anarchists, especially since there were millions of Americans who had never laid eyes on either a Populist or an anarchist. But it was impossible to popularize such a distorted image of the Progressives, who flourished in every section of the country, everywhere visibly, palpably, almost pathetically respectable.—Richard Hofstadter, *The Age of Reform: From Bryan to F.D.R.*, 1955

B: [The] national legislative fruits of the Progressive Era had their unmistakable origins in the agrarian movements of the 1870s, 1880s, and 1890s. Given the indisputable facts of suffrage restriction and resurgent racism, how can we explain the apparent afterlife of populism? . . . There were, in particular, four factors that sustained the agrarian reform program in national politics after 1896: a new wave of farmer organization; the direct primary; the national Democratic Party leadership of William Jennings Bryan; and most fundamentally, regional political economy.—Elizabeth Sanders, *Roots of Reform: Farmers, Workers, and The American State, 1877–1917*, 1999

Explain the differences between Interpretation **A** and Interpretation **B**:

_____

_____

_____

_____

_____

_____

Specific Historical Evidence to Support **A** (not mentioned in passage):

_____

_____

_____

Specific Historical Evidence to Support **B** (not mentioned in passage):

_____

_____

_____

_____

Interpretation: Fundamentalism v. Modernism in the 1920s

A: What harm has the Gospel of Jesus ever done the world? Show me the nation that has ever crumbled into oblivion and decay that was governed by Christian beliefs. Show me the woman who ever became a degenerate or outcast who believed and worshipped God according to His revelation. . . . The burden of proof that the Bible is not the Word of God is on those who reject it, not upon those who receive and believe it. . . . The atheists and agnostics and the materialists must confess that they ought to be able to make a better book, but they have tried time and again, only to fall back hopelessly with despair. Oh, man is growing! The mastery of man's mind over the forces of nature seems almost complete in our day. . . . The great men of the ages are on the side of the Bible.—Billy Sunday, "Nuts for Skeptics to Crack," 1922

B: All modern religions are based, at least on their logical side, on this notion that there are higher powers which observe the doings of man and constantly take a hand in them, and in the fold of Christianity, which is a good deal more sentimental than any other major religion, the concept of interest and intervention is associated with a concept of benevolence. In other words, it is believed that God is predominantly good. No true Christian can tolerate the idea that God ever deliberately and wantonly injures him, or could conceivably wish him ill. The slings and arrows that he suffers, he believes, are brought down upon him by his own ignorance and contumacy. Unhappily, this doctrine of the goodness of God does not fit into what we know of the nature and operations of the cosmos today; it is a survival from a day of universal ignorance. All science is simply a great massing of proofs that God, if He exists, is really neither good nor bad, but simply indifferent—an infinite Force carrying on the operation of unintelligible processes without the slightest regard, either one way or the other, for the comfort, safety and happiness of man.—H.L. Mencken, "High and Ghostly Matters," 1924

Explain the differences between Interpretation **A** and Interpretation **B**:

_____
_____
_____
_____
_____
_____

Specific Historical Evidence to Support **A** (not mentioned in passage):

_____
_____
_____
_____

Specific Historical Evidence to Support **B** (not mentioned in passage):

_____
_____
_____
_____

Interpretation: 1920s

A: For the revolt of the younger generation was only the beginning of a revolution in manners and morals that was already beginning to affect men and women of every age in every part of the country. A number of forces were working together and interacting upon one another to make this revolution inevitable. First of all was the state of mind brought about by the war and it conclusion. . . . The revolution was accelerated also by the growing independence of the American woman. . . . Like all revolutions, this one was stimulated by foreign propaganda. It came, however, not from Moscow, but from Vienna. Sigmund Freud had published his first book on psychoanalysis at the end of the nineteenth century . . . The principal remaining forces which accelerated the revolution in manners and morals were all 100 percent American. They were prohibition, the automobile, the confession and sex magazines, and the movies. . . . Each of these diverse influences . . . was played upon by all the others; none of them could alone have changed to any great degree the folkways of America; together their force was irresistible.—Frederick Lewis Allen, *Only Yesterday*, 1931

B: In its basic patterns, the new ferment of 1920-1924 was far from new. The nativisms that came to the force in 1920 essentially continued prewar trends. They consisted largely of hatreds—toward Catholics, Jews, and southeastern Europeans—that had gathered strength in the late Progressive era, reaching a minor crescendo in 1914. . . . two factors which time and again in American history encouraged anti-foreign outbreaks vividly reappeared. One was economic depression, the other a fresh wave of immigration. . . . Prohibition, however, created a much more highly charged situation, for it precipitated a head-on collision between mounting lawlessness and a new drive for social conformity. . . . In many respects the level of hysteria in the early twenties was a heritage of mind and spirit from the World War. Pre-1914 traditions supplied the massive roots of that hysteria; post-1919 conditions provided fertile soil for a new season of growth; but 100 percent Americanism was the vital force that gave it abundant life.—John Higham, *Strangers in the Land: Patterns of American Nativism, 1860–1925*, 1955

Explain the differences between Interpretation **A** and Interpretation **B**:

_____

_____

_____

_____

_____

Specific Historical Evidence to Support **A** (not mentioned in passage):

_____

_____

_____

Specific Historical Evidence to Support **B** (not mentioned in passage):

_____

_____

_____

Interpretation: Conflict between Science and Theology

A: The first objection to Darwinism is that it is only a guess and was never anything more. . . . The second objection to Darwin's guess is that it has not one syllable in the Bible to support it. This ought to make Christians cautious about accepting it without thorough investigation. . . . Third—Neither Darwin nor his supporters have been able to find a fact in the universe to support their hypothesis. . . . Fourth—Darwinism is not only without foundation, but it compels its believers to resort to explanations that are more absurd than anything found in the "Arabian Nights." . . . The objection to Darwinism is that it is harmful, as well as groundless. It entirely changes one's view of life and undermines faith in the Bible. . . . Anyone desiring to verify these . . . can do so by inquiry at our leading state institutions and even among some of our religious denominational colleges. Fathers and mothers complain of their children losing their interest in religion and speaking lightly of the Bible. . . . The effect of Darwinism is seen in the pulpits; men of prominent denominations deny the virgin birth of Christ and some even His resurrection.—William Jennings Bryan, "God and Evolution," 1922

B: Every universally accepted scientific truth which we possess began as a hypothesis, is in a sense a hypothesis still, and has become a hypothesis transformed into a settled conviction as the mass of accumulating evidence left no questions as to its substantial validity. . . . The fact is that the process by which man came to be upon the planet is a very important scientific problem, but it is not a crucially important religious problem. Origins prove nothing in the realm of values. . . . Our greatest teachers, as well as our poorest, those who are profoundly religious as well as those who are scornfully irreligious, believe in evolution. . . . If the hypothesis of evolution were smashed tomorrow, there would be no more religiously minded scientists and no fewer irreligious ones. . . . scientists will fight against him [i.e., Bryan] in the name of scientific freedom of investigation so will multitudes of Christians fight against him in the name of their religion and their God.—Harry Emerson Fosdick, "A Reply to Mr. Bryan in the Name of Religion," 1922

Explain the differences between Interpretation **A** and Interpretation **B**:

_____

_____

_____

_____

_____

_____

Specific Historical Evidence to Support **A** (not mentioned in passage):

_____

_____

_____

_____

Specific Historical Evidence to Support **B** (not mentioned in passage):

_____

_____

_____

Interpretation: Assessment of the New Deal

A: The very tone of the New Deal was far more aggressively equalitarian than that of either Populism or progressivism. The Populists had never been able to win the workingman; all during the decades from 1865 to 1936, most of the Negroes had been voting Republican while most of the newer immigrants were voting Democratic. The New Deal, for the first time, brought all the low-status groups into one camp and produced an economic and social cleavage in voting unprecedented in the history of the country. Under the circumstances, New Deal liberalism naturally represented leveling to an unusual degree.—Eric F. Goldman, *Rendezvous with Destiny*, 1952

B: When the New Deal was over, capitalism remained intact. The rich still controlled the nation's wealth, as well as its laws, courts, police, newspapers, churches, colleges. Enough help had been given to enough people to make Roosevelt a hero to millions, but the same system that had brought depression and crisis—the system of waste, of inequality, of concern for profit over human need—remained.—Howard Zinn, *A People's History of the United States*, 1980

Explain the differences between Interpretation **A** and Interpretation **B**:

_____

_____

_____

_____

_____

Specific Historical Evidence to Support **A** (not mentioned in passage):

_____

_____

_____

Specific Historical Evidence to Support **B** (not mentioned in passage):

_____

_____

_____

_____

Interpretation: Assessment of the New Deal II

A: The New Deal had performed its necessary tasks well. It kept vital option open in American life. It faced up to an economic crisis that was widening rapidly into a moral and spiritual crisis, and it brought the country through, morally renewed and economically on a far sounder basis. Its accomplishments are so much a part of the landscape today that they twenties have acquired in retrospect the character of fantasy. Perhaps the best evidence of the extent to which the New Deal reshaped American ideas about society is to be found in the evolution of Republican platforms from 1932 to 1948. . . . The New Deal took a broken and despairing land and gave it new confidence in itself. Not perhaps new confidence; but rather a revival of the ancient faith in the free people which, speaking through Jefferson and Jackson and Lincoln, has been our great source of national strength. Roosevelt had a vision of democratic America and the strength to realize a good part of that vision. All his solutions were incomplete. But then all great problems are insoluble. The New Deal left us the fighting spirit and the broad democratic faith in which we may strive to advance the solutions a few steps further.—Arthur M. Schlesinger, Jr., "The Broad Accomplishments of the New Deal," 1948

B: All Roosevelt's promises—to restore purchasing power and mass employment and relieve the needy and aid the farmer and raise agricultural prices and balance the budget and lower the tariff and continue protection— added up to a very discouraging performance to those who hoped for a coherent liberal program. . . . The New Deal will never be understood by anyone who looks for a single thread of policy, a far-reaching, far-seeing plan. It was a series of improvisations, many adopted very suddenly, many contradictory. Such unity as it has was in political strategy, not economics. . . . The New Deal had accomplished a heart-warming relief of distress, it had achieved a certain measure of recovery . . . But, as Roosevelt was aware, it had failed to realize his objectives of distributive justice and sound, stable prosperity. . . . What would have happened to the political fortunes of Franklin D. Roosevelt if the war had not created a new theater for his leadership?—Richard Hofstadter, *The American Political Tradition and the Men Who Made It*, 1948

Explain the differences between Interpretation **A** and Interpretation **B**:

_____

_____

_____

_____

_____

_____

Specific Historical Evidence to Support **A** (not mentioned in passage):

_____

_____

_____

Specific Historical Evidence to Support **B** (not mentioned in passage):

_____

_____

_____

_____

Interpretation: McCarthyism

A: Like him or not, it is generally acknowledged that Joe McCarthy is the most controversial figure that American politics has thrown up since F.D.R. His ill-wishers have watched him with keyhole intentness to catch him in a slip, but he has brilliantly baffled them. His admirers are a growing and dedicated company. Within the Republican Party, McCarthy's position is strategic. After Eisenhower, he looms as the only Republican who commands a great following among the Democrats. . . . McCarthy is where he is today because he satisfies the deep national hunger for an affirmative man. . . . McCarthy, although he has made mistakes, has never made the ineffable mistake of wearing the people. . . . As Russia and Red China advance nightmarishly toward the maximum power goals which they will reach in the nineteen seventies, the American people will be as unlikely to think seriously of anything else, as to ignore an onrushing comet. . . . McCarthy is the articulate voice of the American people in a Communist-haunted age. On this issue, he marches with history. He cannot lose.—Harold Lord Varney, "What Has Joe McCarthy Accomplished?" 1954

B: It is possible, of course, to say that the McCarthy years were only a rather dramatic episode in a broad and continuing historical movement. He shook the entire tree, not just the political limbs. Many of the nonpolitical limbs proved weak. . . . However that may be, we are faced with the fact that he gave the tree one hell of a shaking. It did not fall, and he did, but we cannot put aside our memories of the day when fifty per cent of the people had a "favorable opinion" of this bully and fraud . . . There must be grave risks in any open society . . . grave risks make life worth living. McCarthy offered a powerful challenge to freedom, and he showed us to be more vulnerable than many of us had guessed to a seditious demagogy—as well as less vulnerable than some of us feared.—Richard H. Rovere, *Senator Joe McCarthy*, 1959

Explain the differences between Interpretation **A** and Interpretation **B**:

_____

_____

_____

_____

_____

Specific Historical Evidence to Support **A** (not mentioned in passage):

_____

_____

_____

_____

Specific Historical Evidence to Support **B** (not mentioned in passage):

_____

_____

_____

_____

Interpretation: Growth of Urbanization

A: I wish to give you some reasons why a great city is a great evil. . . . In the city, and most of the great cities are crowded, there must be less oxygen and more microbes. . . . It is a great evil in the city that people are cut off from nature . . . It is an evil in that it separates the greater part of the community into classes and disturbs the sentiment of neighborliness between the richer and the poorer, which existed formerly in smaller communities, and which ought to exist. . . . Life in the great city tends to stimulate and increase beyond measure that which is the menace of the American city—intensification of nervous strain and nervous excitability . . . they are particularly unfavorable for the . . . boys and girls. . . . Great cities are liable to become great dangers in a political sense, because the more men are crowded in great masses . . . the more they form what might be called a revolutionary temper . . . In the great city there is a deplorable amount of economic waste.—James Bryce, "The Menace of Great Cities," 1912

B: The twentieth century opens with two distinguishing features—the dominant city and militant democracy. . . . The city may change in many ways—undoubtedly it will. In the city of ten or possibly twenty million people there will be a redistribution of centers, possibly a re-division of political functions. But, in a historical sense, the city has resumed the commanding position which it enjoyed in the days of Athens, Rome, and the medieval towns. . . . The features common to both are a close association of mankind with many cooperative activities. Nor does the analogy stop here, for in every age the great cities of the world have enjoyed a certain degree of freedom; of local control over the conduct of their affairs. . . . The great difference between the twentieth-century city and those of the past lies in our legalized freedom; in universal education; in an organized machinery backed by years of tradition; but especially in the social instincts and industrial background of the present. Democracy, rather than class or business interest, is becoming intelligently organized. In this respect the twentieth century marks the dawning of an epoch in Western civilization.—Frederic C. Howe, *The City: The Hope of Democracy*, 1909

Explain the differences between Interpretation **A** and Interpretation **B**:

_____

_____

_____

_____

_____

_____

Specific Historical Evidence to Support **A** (not mentioned in passage):

_____

_____

_____

Specific Historical Evidence to Support **B** (not mentioned in passage):

_____

_____

_____

Interpretation: Foundations of Postwar Conservatism

A: Groups of predominantly white, middle, and upper-class wives and mothers took advantage of their privileged social circumstances to become militant anticommunist crusaders. . . . we see that women's clubs were important incubators of McCarthyism and that housewife activists played a critical role in mobilizing the grassroots base of the conservative movement. The postwar revival of domesticity created new opportunities for women to leverage gender norms in politics. The heightened concerns over brainwashing, mind control, and indoctrination invited conservative women to become political right where they were: in PTA meetings, church groups, and their homes. Postwar domesticity also breathed new life into notions of women's moral superiority. The threat of "Godless" communism gave women a mandate to become more assertive in their roles as the upholders of spiritual and civil virtues. . . . Patriotic bookstores, most of which were created and staffed by women, were some of the earliest signs of conservatism's growing strength . . . . The bookstores, like the anticommunist study clubs and investigative committees, illustrate the extent to which postwar domesticity had an impact on the conservative movement.—Michelle Nickerson, "Women, Domesticity, and Postwar Conservatism," 2003

B: The Christian Right is a social movement that seeks to mobilize and represent evangelical Christians in politics. . . . even as the Christian Right of the 1950s faded away, the religious conservatives that served as their target constituency continued to build infrastructure—Bible colleges, Christian bookstores, and specialized magazines and newspapers. . . . In the late 1970s, Republican activists helped provide resources to form yet another wave of fundamentalist political groups. . . . Many of these activists worked to gain influence in and even control of state and local party committees. These activists provided a core of skilled political workers ready to enlist in the next Christian Right crusade.—Clyde Wilcox, "Laying Up Treasures in Washington and in Heaven: The Christian Right and Evangelical Politics in the Twentieth Century and Beyond," 2003

Explain the differences between Interpretation **A** and Interpretation **B**:

_____

_____

_____

_____

_____

_____

Specific Historical Evidence to Support **A** (not mentioned in passage):

_____

_____

_____

_____

Specific Historical Evidence to Support **B** (not mentioned in passage):

_____

_____

_____

_____

Interpretation: NATO and Containment

A: NATO had, as a military alliance, its part to play; but I think everyone of us hoped that its purely military role would decline in importance as the curse of bipolarity fell from the Continent, as negotiations took place, as armies were withdrawn, as the contest of ideologies took other forms. The central agency in this concept was not NATO but the European Recovery Program . . . I should like to raise today the question whether anything has really happened to invalidate this original concept on which both Marshall Plan and NATO were founded, whether the positive goals of Western policy have really receded so far from the range of practical possibility as to be considered eclipsed by the military danger, whether we would not, in fact, be safer and better off today if we could put our military fixations aside . . . [this] would not imply, first of all, that military strength would not continue to be cultivated on our side until we have better alternatives. . . . . [but] NATO must not be strengthened in such a way as to prejudice the chances for an eventual reduction, by peaceful negotiation, of the danger of an all-out war.—George F. Kennan, *Russia, the Atom and the West*, 1958

B: [The] foreign policy of the United States has become, by necessity, a positive and activist one . . . . The evils of a timid and defeatist policy of retreat are far deeper than its ineptness as a move in the propaganda battle. It would abandon the efforts of a decade . . . A strong united Europe could have the men and the resources—along with British and United States contingents—to deal by conventional forces with invasion by conventional forces, particularly as the Eastern European satellites are becoming a danger, and not an asset, to Soviet military power. This, if pressed, gives real mutuality of benefit to a negotiated reduction in forces. It makes possible, too, a time when nuclear forces would no longer have to be relied on as a substitute for conventional forces, and with it a real opportunity to negotiate this threat further and further into the background.—Dean Acheson, "The Illusion of Disengagement," 1958

Explain the differences between Interpretation **A** and Interpretation **B**:

_____

_____

_____

_____

_____

_____

Specific Historical Evidence to Support **A** (not mentioned in passage):

_____

_____

_____

_____

Specific Historical Evidence to Support **B** (not mentioned in passage):

_____

_____

_____

_____

Interpretation: Sit-In Movement

A: Direct action is not a substitute for work in the courts and the halls of government. Bringing about the passage of a new and broad law by a city council, state legislature or the Congress, or pleading cases before the courts of the land, does not eliminate the necessity for bringing about the mass dramatization of injustice in front of a city hall. Indeed, direct action and legal action complement one another, when skillfully employed, each becomes more effective. The chronology of the sit-ins confirms this observation. Spontaneously born, but guided by the theory of nonviolent resistance, the lunch-counter sit-ins accomplished integration in hundreds of communities at the swiftest rate of change in the civil rights movement up to that time. . . . As a consequence of combining direct and legal action, far-reaching precedents were established, which served, in turn, to extend the areas of desegregation.—Martin Luther King, Jr., *Why We Can't Wait*, 1964

B: A lot of people, Black and white, have the impression that those of us who got involved in the Movement, when it started in 1960, were fighting for integration. That's the way the white press interpreted the sit-ins and freedom rides and all that. But what they didn't understand was that none of us was concerned about sitting down next to a white man and eating a hamburger. Anybody who thinks that is reflecting white nationalism. That's a white supremacist attitude. . . . Integration was never our concern. In fact, integration is impractical. You cannot legislate an attitude, and integration is based upon an attitude of mutual acceptance and respect between two racial or cultural groups in the society. . . . what the Civil Rights Movement was concerned with was controlling the animalistic behavior of white people. . . . We were letting white folks know that they could no longer legislate where we went or what we did.—H. Rap Brown, *Die Nigger Die*, 1969

Explain the differences between Interpretation **A** and Interpretation **B**:

_____

_____

_____

_____

_____

_____

Specific Historical Evidence to Support **A** (not mentioned in passage):

_____

_____

_____

Specific Historical Evidence to Support **B** (not mentioned in passage):

_____

_____

_____

Interpretation: 1960s

A: The liberal democratic state has accomplished two things in particular. It has brought about a redistribution of wealth which has defeated Marx's prediction of progressive immiseration; and it has brought about an economic stabilization which has defeated Marx's prediction of ever-worsening economic crisis. What the democratic parties of the developed nations have done . . . to control the business cycle and to reapportion income in favor of those whom Jackson called the "humble members of society." . . . The problems of the New Deal were essentially quantitative problems—problems meeting stark human needs for food, clothing, shelter and employment. Most of these needs are now effectively met for most Americans; but a sense of spiritual disquietude remains nevertheless. . . . The final lesson of the affluent society is surely that affluence is not enough—that solving the quantitative problems of living only increases the importance of the quality of the life lived . . . These qualitative problems seem next on the American agenda.—Arthur M. Schlesinger, Jr., *The Vital Center*, 1977

B: The heyday of the counter culture coincided with the buildup of the Vietnam War . . . It also coincided with the climax of racial confrontation . . . [but] the actual process of recruitment to the counter culture probably owed more to three factors that had little enough to do with politics except as symbols—to drugs, to rock music, and to the underground media . . . The years from 1965 to 1968 were years of polarization for America partly because they were years of unit for the counter culture. . . . Indeed, the cultural revolutionaries and the political radicals often were the same people, in the beginning. They had a single enemy, as they saw it in the first, innocent days, whether they called it capitalism, or the System, or Pig Nation, or Amerika . . . In political terms, the counter culture's claim to be revolutionary was always tenuous. Even in its political aspect, it was a subjective culture, more interested in the ethics and feelings of its member than in changing the outside world. . . . They turned to the life style of the counter culture for all the things they had missed in the sheltered, affluent suburbs where they grew up: excitement, purpose, a feeling of community, and some measure of individual worth.—Godfrey Hodgson, *America in our Time*, 1976

Explain the differences between Interpretation **A** and Interpretation **B**:

_____

_____

_____

_____

_____

_____

Specific Historical Evidence to Support **A** (not mentioned in passage):

_____

_____

_____

Specific Historical Evidence to Support **B** (not mentioned in passage):

_____

_____

_____

_____

Interpretation: 1980s

A: Frustrated by the failure of government policy, critics from the right and the left—for decidedly different reasons—joined in denouncing the liberal vision. . . . Convinced of the inadequacies of federal programs, political activists turned increasingly to more manageable arenas—state, local, and neighborhood organizations. . . . The belief in community democracy encouraged the proliferation of grass-roots organizations that worked for social betterment. . . . This burgeoning dissent awakened public suspicions, reminiscent of the antiwar movement, about government credibility . . . The repudiation of liberalism by community populists paralleled a reinvigorated attack on the same system by its traditional enemies—the conservative right. . . . The New Right ironically drew strength from social discontents similar in some ways to those that motivated community populists—a distrust of liberal economics and the expansion of government bureaucracy. . . . The celebration of the old American values coincided with an impassioned effort by the New Right to restore an old moral order.—Peter N. Carroll, *It Seemed Like Nothing Happened: The Tragedy and Promise of America in the 1970s*, 1982

B: Travelers crossing the United States by automobile in the late 1970s could hardly fail to be impressed by the evidence of regional homogeneity. Driving along highways commonly known by numbers rather than by names—Interstate 80, for example . . . they could stop to eat almost anywhere at a Kentucky Fried Chicken franchise or a McDonald's outlet and would discover, where they were, that one drumstick or hamburger tasted exactly like another. . . . Behind the appearance of uniformity, however, differences along class, racial, and ethnic lines persisted. While they had changed dramatically over a forty-year period, these distinctions continued to shape the lives of most Americans. . . . The preacher's cry in Ecclesiastes—"There is no new thing under the sun"—should be taken not as witness to the immutability of class, racial, and ethnic patters but as testament to their enduring influence.—Richard Polenberg, *One Nation Divisible*, 1980

Explain the differences between Interpretation **A** and Interpretation **B**:

_____

_____

_____

_____

_____

_____

Specific Historical Evidence to Support **A** (not mentioned in passage):

_____

_____

_____

_____

Specific Historical Evidence to Support **B** (not mentioned in passage):

_____

_____

_____

_____

Interpretation: End of the Cold War

A: The way the Cold War ended . . . was directly related to the way in which it had begun. . . . the struggle really was, ultimately, about two ways of life, one that abandoned freedom in its effort to rationalize politics, and another that was content to leave politics as the irrational process that it normally is, thereby preserving freedom. The idea of freedom proved more durable than the practice of authoritarianism, and as a consequence, the Cold War ended. . . . It is important to remember, though, that the peaceful end to the Cold War we have just witnessed is not the only conceivable way the Cold War could have ended. In adding up that conflict's costs, we would do well to recognize that the time it took to conclude the struggle was not time entirely wasted. That time—and those costs—appear to us excessive in retrospect, but future historians may see those expenditures as long-term investments in ensuring that the Cold War ended peacefully. For what we wound up doing with nuclear weapons was buying time—the time necessary for the authoritarian approach to politics to defeat itself by non-military means. And the passage of time, even if purchased at an exorbitant price has at last begun to pay dividends.—John Lewis Gaddis, "The Cold War, the Long Peace, and the Future," 1992

B: Now with the Cold War behind us, can it truly be said that we passed this test? . . . Too often both leaders and the public were willing to compromise American principles and ideals (not to mention law) in the name of fighting communism. The United States emerged from the Cold War over-armed, burdened by debt and poverty, and carrying numerous scars from self-inflicted wounds to cherished institutions—all for the sake of the superpower competition. In forging itself into a hard-line Cold War warrior, the U.S. ultimately undermined its "best traditions" more than it measured up to them. Had its leaders and citizens demonstrated greater faith in the strength of the nation's founding principles, the U.S. might have emerged from the Cold War contest economically leaner, brighter of spirit, and with its democratic institutions and values far stronger.—Wade Huntley, "Who Won the Cold War?," 1993

Explain the differences between Interpretation **A** and Interpretation **B**:

_____

_____

_____

_____

_____

_____

Specific Historical Evidence to Support **A** (not mentioned in passage):

_____

_____

_____

Specific Historical Evidence to Support **B** (not mentioned in passage):

_____

_____

_____

_____

Student Instructions: Chronological Reasoning

When we are asked to use chronological reasoning, we place a variety of events in historical order. Although it might not seem important to know historical dates, the reality is that dates help us to conceptualize important trends. Understanding when and why things occurred is critical to understanding history. It would be impossible to practice many, if not all, of the historical thinking skills without the proper chronology of content.

The purpose of the Chronological Reasoning graphic organizers is not only to practice placing a number of historical events in the correct order but also to understand how and why things occurred based on that order. For example, you may be asked to apply this historical skill to the Early National or Antebellum periods. This practice will help reinforce your knowledge of the given historical period and will encourage you to think about how these events relate to each other.

At the top of each of these graphic organizers, you will be provided with 15 events. The specific events are jumbled up in no particular order. Notice on the sample provided that the date of each event is written next to it. It is strongly recommended that you write in the dates when completing these graphic organizers, because doing so will help you place them in chronological order. You then will select 10 events to put in chronological order on the left side. The lines next to these events are where you will demonstrate your ability to connect the different events, describing them and determining their causes and effects.

Chronological Reasoning: Rise of Nationalism

Jay's Treaty 1794	Somerset Case 1772
Articles of Confederation ratified 1781	Louisiana Purchase 1803
War of 1812 1812	Inauguration of Adams 1797
Northwest Ordinance 1787	Hartford Convention 1814
XYZ Affair 1798	Bill of Rights ratified 1791
Neutrality Proclamation 1793	Embargo Act 1807
Shays's Rebellion 1786	Inauguration of Washington 1789
Prohibition of slave trade 1808	

1st EVENT   _Articles of Conferation_

2nd EVENT   _Shays's Rebellion_

3rd EVENT   _Northwest Ordinance_

4th EVENT   _Inauguration of Washington_

5th EVENT   _Bill of Rights_

6th EVENT   _Neutrality Proclamation_

7th EVENT   _Jay's Treaty_

8th EVENT   _Inauguration of Adams_

9th EVENT   _XYZ Affair_

10th EVENT   _War of 1812_

The first constitution of America had weaknesses, and the main criticism of the government was that it could not deal with internal rebellions like Shays's Rebellion. The Articles of Confederation did have some positives though—passage of both the Land Ordinance and the Northwest Ordinance dealt with the northwest territory. Eventually the Articles of Confederation gave way to a stronger federal government, and the country saw the ratification of the U.S. Constitution and the inauguration of the first president—George Washington. The debate over the ratification centered around the adoption of the Bill of Rights. Two major issues in Washington's administration concerned issues with the French and the British. The treaty with France, over opposition by the Jeffersonian Republicans, was nullified by the Neutrality Proclamation. Hamilton stressed the importance of continued trade with Britain, and the country entered into a treaty with the countries' leading partner, Jay's Treaty. Washington set the two-term limit, and his vice-president, John Adams, became the second president. Because of the treaty with Britain, the French wanted their own treaty so Adams sent delegates, who were rebuffed, which resulted in the XYZ Affair. The continued impressments of American sailors by the British led to the War of 1812.

Chronological Reasoning: Colonial America

Founding of Massachusetts	First Navigation Act
Seven Years' War	Albany Plan of Union
Great Migration	First Great Awakening
Pontiac's Rebellion	Founding of Jamestown
Founding of Maryland	Walking Purchase
King Philip's War	Salem Witch Trials
Bacon's Rebellion	Zenger Trial
Half-Way Covenant	

1st EVENT _____ _____

2nd EVENT _____ _____

3rd EVENT _____ _____

4th EVENT _____ _____

5th EVENT _____ _____

6th EVENT _____ _____

7th EVENT _____ _____

8th EVENT _____ _____

9th EVENT _____ _____

10th EVENT _____ _____

Chronological Reasoning: American Revolution

Bill for Establishing Religious Freedom	Publication of *The Wealth of Nations*
Battle of Saratoga	Vermont bans slavery
Intolerable Acts	Battles of Lexington and Concord
Treaty of Paris	First Continental Congress convenes
Townshend Acts	Boston Massacre
Phillipsburgh Proclamation	Declaration of Independence
First National Census	*Common Sense* published
Stamp Act Congress	

1st EVENT _____ _____

_____

2nd EVENT _____ _____

_____

3rd EVENT _____ _____

_____

4th EVENT _____ _____

_____

5th EVENT _____ _____

_____

6th EVENT _____ _____

_____

7th EVENT _____ _____

_____

8th EVENT _____ _____

_____

9th EVENT _____ _____

_____

10th EVENT _____ _____

Chronological Reasoning: Early 19th Century

Indian Removal Act	Nullification Crisis
Second Great Awakening	Second Bank of the United States
Monroe Doctrine	Fulton's Steamboat navigates the Hudson
Economic Panic	River
Trail of Tears	Manifest Destiny coined
Invention of the Cotton Gin	Telegraph invented
Adams-Onis Treaty	Missouri Compromise
Dartmouth College v. Woodward	Dorr War

1st EVENT _____   _____

2nd EVENT _____   _____

3rd EVENT _____   _____

4th EVENT _____   _____

5th EVENT _____   _____

6th EVENT _____   _____

7th EVENT _____   _____

8th EVENT _____   _____

9th EVENT _____   _____

10th EVENT _____   _____

Chronological Reasoning: Reform Movements

Female Moral Reform Society organized	Brook Farm established
Denmark Vessy's slave conspiracy	*The Liberator* first published
American Colonization Society founded	*Uncle Tom's Cabin* published
Harriet Tubman escapes slavery	*An Appeal to the Colored Citizens of*
Nat Turner's Rebellion	*the World* published
Gabriel's Rebellion	Slave uprising on the Creole
American Temperance Society founded	American Anti-slavery Society founded
Seneca Falls Convention	Great Britain abolishes slavery

1ˢᵗ EVENT _____ _____

_____

2ⁿᵈ EVENT _____ _____

_____

3ʳᵈ EVENT _____ _____

_____

4ᵗʰ EVENT _____ _____

_____

5ᵗʰ EVENT _____ _____

_____

6ᵗʰ EVENT _____ _____

_____

7ᵗʰ EVENT _____ _____

_____

8ᵗʰ EVENT _____ _____

_____

9ᵗʰ EVENT _____ _____

_____

10ᵗʰ EVENT _____ _____

Chronological Reasoning: Civil War Era

Bleeding Kansas	Kansas-Nebraska Act
Emancipation Proclamation	Mexican-American War
Inauguration of Hayes	Ku Klux Klan established
Assassination of Lincoln	Wilmot Proviso
Fugitive Slave Acts	Dred Scott decision
Homestead Act	First Battle of Bull Run
13th Amendment	Feminist organization splits
National economic depression	

1st EVENT   _____   _____

                                    _____

2nd EVENT   _____   _____

                                    _____

3rd EVENT   _____   _____

                                    _____

4th EVENT   _____   _____

                                    _____

5th EVENT   _____   _____

                                    _____

6th EVENT   _____   _____

                                    _____

7th EVENT   _____   _____

                                    _____

8th EVENT   _____   _____

                                    _____

9th EVENT   _____   _____

                                    _____

10th EVENT   _____   _____

Chronological Reasoning: America in the Gilded Age

Dawes Act	*Lochner v. New York*
Sherman Anti-trust Act	Spanish-American War
Homestead Strike	Great Railroad Strike
Gold Standard Act	Pullman Strike
Haymarket Affair	Interstate Commerce Commission created
Reconstruction Ends	Insular cases
Chinese Exclusion Act	*Plessy v. Ferguson*
Populist Party organized	

1st EVENT _____ _____
_____

2nd EVENT _____ _____
_____

3rd EVENT _____ _____
_____

4th EVENT _____ _____
_____

5th EVENT _____ _____
_____

6th EVENT _____ _____
_____

7th EVENT _____ _____
_____

8th EVENT _____ _____
_____

9th EVENT _____ _____
_____

10th EVENT _____ _____

Chronological Reasoning: Early 20th Century

Fourteen Points	United States enters WWI
Formation of the Industrial Workers of the World	Espionage Act
	Scopes Trial
Sacco and Vanzetti trial	Northern Securities dissolved
Stock Market crashes	Hawley-Smoot Tariff
Hull House	*The Jungle* published
Pure Food and Drug Act	Clayton Anti-trust Act
Roosevelt Corollary	Gentlemen's Agreement

1st EVENT _____   _____

_____

2nd EVENT _____   _____

_____

3rd EVENT _____   _____

_____

4th EVENT _____   _____

_____

5th EVENT _____   _____

_____

6th EVENT _____   _____

_____

7th EVENT _____   _____

_____

8th EVENT _____   _____

_____

9th EVENT _____   _____

_____

10th EVENT _____   _____

Chronological Reasoning: Depression, New Deal, and WWII

Neutrality Act	Fair Labor Standards Bill
The Hundred Days Congress	Munich Agreement
Smith Act	Yalta Conference
Atlantic Charter	Zoot Suit Riots
GI Bill of Rights	Second New Deal
21st Amendment	Scottsboro Case
Indian Reorganization Act	Exclusion Act
Lend-Lease Act	

1st EVENT _____ _____

2nd EVENT _____ _____

3rd EVENT _____ _____

4th EVENT _____ _____

5th EVENT _____ _____

6th EVENT _____ _____

7th EVENT _____ _____

8th EVENT _____ _____

9th EVENT _____ _____

10th EVENT _____ _____

Chronological Reasoning: Cold War

Truman Doctrine	Federal Interstate Highway Act
Korean War	National Defense Education Act
NSC-68	Army–McCarthy hearings
Earl Warren	*Brown v. Board of Education*
Geneva Accords	Montgomery Bus Boycott
Taft-Hartley Act	North Atlantic Treaty Organization
Marshall Plan	Eisenhower Doctrine
Sputnik launched	

1st EVENT _____   _____

_____

2nd EVENT _____   _____

_____

_____

3rd EVENT _____   _____

_____

4th EVENT _____   _____

_____

5th EVENT _____   _____

_____

6th EVENT _____   _____

_____

7th EVENT _____   _____

_____

8th EVENT _____   _____

_____

9th EVENT _____   _____

_____

10th EVENT _____   _____

Chronological Reasoning: Late 20th Century

Voting Rights Act	Watergate scandal
Tet Offensive	Sagebrush Rebellion
Freedom Rides	Alliance for Progress
Roe v. Wade	Kennedy assassinated
My Lai Massacre	Title IX
The Feminine Mystique published	War Powers Act
SALT signed	Reagan elected
Iran-Contra Affair	

1st EVENT _____ _____

_____

2nd EVENT _____ _____

_____

3rd EVENT _____ _____

_____

4th EVENT _____ _____

_____

5th EVENT _____ _____

_____

6th EVENT _____ _____

_____

7th EVENT _____ _____

_____

8th EVENT _____ _____

_____

9th EVENT _____ _____

_____

10th EVENT _____ _____

Chronological Reasoning: Modern America

Oslo Accords	Kyoto Protocol
Gulf War	Hurricane Katrina
North American Free Trade Agreement	Panamanian Coup
World Trade Center bombed	Clinton impeached
Operation Enduring Freedom	USA Patriot Act
Operation Iraqi Freedom	Department of Homeland Security
Germany reunites	Great Recession begins
Disabilities Act	

1st EVENT _____ _____

2nd EVENT _____ _____

3rd EVENT _____ _____

4th EVENT _____ _____

5th EVENT _____ _____

6th EVENT _____ _____

7th EVENT _____ _____

8th EVENT _____ _____

9th EVENT _____ _____

10th EVENT _____ _____